D1405260

Resources for Differentiated Instruction

BOOK 3

Strategies for English-Language Learners

Copyright © 2005, 2003 by Scholastic Inc.

All rights reserved.   Published by Scholastic Inc.   Printed in the U.S.A.

ISBN 0-439-67067-5

SCHOLASTIC, READ 180, rBOOK, SCHOLASTIC RED, SCHOLASTIC ACHIEVEMENT MANAGER, SCHOLASTIC READING INVENTORY, SCHOLASTIC READING COUNTS!, and associated logos and designs are trademarks and/or registered trademarks of Scholastic Inc. LEXILE and LEXILE FRAMEWORK are registered trademarks of MetaMetrics, Inc.

4 5 6 7 8 9 10   14   14 13 12 11 10 09 08 07 06

Contents

Language Development Activities

Resources

Introduction to *Strategies for English-Language Learners*

Overview

Strategies for English-Language Learners provides oral language activities and introductory reading and writing activities for English-language learners to make a smooth transition into *READ 180* and move towards greater proficiency.

• **Activities** Fifty classroom-tested activities focus on listening and speaking skills. They provide context-based, engaging ways for English-language learners—as well as native speakers—to build oral vocabulary and develop an ear for English-language conventions. These activities include steps and Additional Practice strategies that may be used repeatedly with different examples or in different contexts to address reading and writing proficiency.

Professional Development and Additional Resources

• **Red Professional Development** The following articles provide research-based background information and practical day-to-day tips for integrating English-language learner materials into your instructional plans.

> **"*READ 180* and the English-Language Learner,"** by Alma Corona, presents classroom-tested strategies and ideas for teaching ELL students in the *READ 180* classroom. (See **page 8.**)

> **"Language Development,"** by Jo Gusman, provides research-based background information and practical teaching suggestions. (See **page 10.**)

> **"Software Support for the English-Language Learner"** presents a short, easy-to-use technical guide to customizing the *READ 180* Software for ELL students. (See **page 18.**)

• **Community Builders** Use these activities to break the ice and get students started listening and speaking to one another. The peer interview and personal interest forms help build familiarity and a sense of community among students. (See **pages 71–76.**)

Use these tips to get started quickly:

1. Become familiar with Red Professional Development, **pages 8–19.** As you read, consider specific goals and your plans for meeting them. Record ideas and best practices, or note discussion points. (See Implementing Best Practices for English-Language Learners, **page 7.**)

2. Build community as early in the year as possible. Help students become oriented and feel comfortable. (See How to Use Community Builders, **page 71.**)

3. Preview activities and select those best suited to your students.

4. Invite student participation with encouragement and support.

Classroom Management

Use these activities to differentiate instruction after *rBook* Checkpoints or during other breaks from *rBook* instruction. All of the activities in this book are designed for use as needed to complement the unique organization of the *READ 180* classroom, during Whole- or Small-Group Instruction.

• **Whole-Group Instruction** If a large number of your students are English-language learners, the activities in this book provide great ways to start each day and get students on track. Keep in mind that these activities are intended for all students who could benefit from oral-language practice, including those whose first language is English.

• **Small-Group Instruction** You may wish to group English-language learners together and use these language activities during Small-Group Instruction. The activities are designed so that they may be completed in approximately 20 minutes.

• **Selecting Appropriate Activities** The oral-language development activities cover a wide range of contexts and skills. They do not need to be completed in order. Rather, choose activities that are appropriate to your students' proficiency levels and instructional needs. The Table of Contents and Index are useful references for your choices. To keep a record of lessons students have completed, you may wish to use the Activity Tracking Chart. (See **page 74.**)

• **Objectives and TESOL Standards** Select activities to use at different times based on varied instructional goals, including specific objectives and TESOL Standards.

Oral Language Instruction and Practice

The activities are easy to use and flexible. Each activity is structured as follows:

• **Build Background** The first part of the activity introduces a skill or concept, providing background about language concepts such as: *What is rhyme? What is a command? What is a tongue twister?* This quick review of the key concept is not intended to offer thorough instruction of the skill. If you find that a topic is too challenging for students, you may wish to reteach that skill or to skip to a different activity entirely. In this way, Build Background helps you establish the appropriate level of instruction for your students.

• **Demonstrate** Use examples from the Idea Bank to model skills and explain to students how the skill or activity works. Be sure to engage all the students in the demonstration and to monitor their understanding whenever possible by:

  • **asking questions.**

  • **rehearsing.**

  • **having partners with diverse proficiency work together.**

  • **getting feedback from students after each activity.**

(Continued on next page)

- **Monitor Progress** Monitor students as they complete the activities, checking that they understand and can perform the tasks required, and provide assistance as needed. Encourage students to support one another by helping classmates feel confident as they practice new skills, demonstrate creativity, and participate fully in the activities.

- **Reteach** The Idea Bank in each activity offers additional examples for students to practice and reinforce skills. Select examples that are most appropriate for your students' levels. Feel free to add your own ideas. You also may wish to use these ideas to reteach the concept at another time.

- **Modify** The Modifications section offers ideas that support students with greater or lesser proficiency. You may find the modification ideas useful in providing extra challenges to students.

Implementing Best Practices for English-Language Learners

Use this page to keep track of important ideas as you read Red Professional Development, **pages 8–19.**

Key Points	How I Will Use in Classroom
1.	
2.	
3.	
4.	
5.	
6.	
7.	
8.	
9.	
10.	

Value Student Contributions

Take advantage of the different sets of knowledge and skills ELL students bring to the classroom.

- Encourage peer support.
- Survey students' background knowledge and build on it when introducing new material, integrating students' cultures and experiences.
- Acknowledge the role of "translator" that ELL students often take on for family and other classmates.
- Allow time for reflection in journals or in class discussions.
- Record students' progress so that they can see their own improvement.
- Be sure to keep parents informed of students' progress, and make a special point of noting improvements.

READ 180 and the English-Language Learner

by Alma O. Corona

Organize your classroom and plan lessons to best meet the needs of your English-language learners.

Introducing *READ 180*

Introducing the program to students is necessary in any *READ 180* classroom, but it's particularly important for ELL students. These students are encountering new words, environments, and ideas at a daunting rate. Before students arrive, make sure that the classroom is organized and welcoming. Some ways that you can do this follow:

- Clearly identify each learning station.
- Explain instructions to students and check for comprehension by questioning and having students restate important ideas.
- Arrange materials so that they are accessible to students.
- Use a timer to monitor time for the various activities.
- Set up portfolios in which students may keep their work.

When students arrive, explain the program to them. This includes familiarizing them with the various materials, such as the Paperbacks and Audiobooks. Allow time for students to explore the Software.

Finally, grouping ELL students heterogeneously allows for greater success in reading comprehension by enhancing peer relations and self-confidence. Inside diverse groups, students with different English-language abilities will feel included and valued.

In addition, you may wish to organize a *READ 180* night to introduce the program to students' families.

SCHOLASTIC
red. Faculty

Alma O. Corona is certified in both bilingual and special education. She has been teaching for over 12 years in the South Bay Union School District, San Diego, California. She presently serves more than 130 *READ 180* students at Mendoza Elementary School.

Whole-Group and Small-Group Instruction

Lesson Planning Use these suggestions to address ELL students' needs:

- Limit the number of key points in any one lesson. Find a memorable way to signal key points. This will help students focus on important information.

- Break up lessons into smaller parts to provide greater in-depth discussion. This can include identifying and numbering paragraphs to facilitate student discussion.

- Choose literature with cultural relevance for ELL students at their appropriate Lexile® level.

- Build on student knowledge by bridging new lessons to previously taught lessons. Present all information in a meaningful context.

- Provide students with opportunities to extend their oral-language proficiency by using the suggestions for reading and writing that appear in the activities.

- Correct work completed during Small-Group Instruction with students. Doing so will allow you to offer individualized instruction to the ELL student and is another opportunity to review the material.

Lesson Delivery Use the following strategies to make lessons accessible to ELL students:

- Use multimedia manipulatives (audio and visual).

- Phrase questions so that ELL students have a chance to respond by pointing or using one-word answers.

- Limit the amount of extraneous language you use during explanations. Students who are struggling with English will strain after every word, and may lack the ability to distinguish between important points and personal asides.

- If necessary, offer a verbal alternative to written responses, such as QuickWrites. Support students by allowing them to dictate to you. Paraphrase and elaborate on their responses to help them express their ideas.

- To maximize language development and build content-area vocabulary, use discussions, graphic organizers, illustrations, and concrete examples.

Multisensory Techniques ELL students can benefit from teaching that involves their senses and imagination. This type of teaching not only finds a way around language limitations, but it can enliven the classroom and spark students' interest. The following are some ideas of this type of teaching:

- Role-play wherever possible.

- Incorporate objects that students can see, hear, touch, smell, or taste. Use of visuals, music, and nature can all help you demonstrate concepts without using words. For example, to demonstrate a difficult concept such as condensation, begin by having students breathe on a mirror.

- Allow students to express ideas using poetry, dancing, singing, and drawing.

Emphasis on Vocabulary ELL students will benefit from increased time on vocabulary and word study activities. Some effective teaching techniques follow:

- Introduce and preteach the vocabulary used in *READ 180* readings to expand reading comprehension.

- Give examples of new vocabulary by using synonyms and providing examples in meaningful, culturally relevant context whenever possible.

- Expand students' vocabulary by teaching synonyms, antonyms, prefixes, suffixes, and root/base words in meaningful, relevant contexts.

- Model word pronunciation and spelling.

- Provide dictionaries (picture dictionaries, if possible) and thesauruses. Bilingual dictionaries offer first-language support.

What Research Says

- A nonthreatening and affirming environment is vital for students to learn (Krashen, 1985).

- The process of language acquisition is predictable, but the rate varies depending on the individual (Cummins, 1994).

- Language learners acquire language that expresses basic needs first and content-area concepts later (Cummins, 1994).

- Language learners look and listen for recognizable patterns made understandable by the context (Helman, 2004).

- Teachers can use strategies to make language accessible and encourage the process of language development (Sarosy & Sherak, 2002).

Language Development

by Jo Gusman

An expert in the field, Jo Gusman shares research and practical ideas for language development.

My Personal Experience

I began my journey by walking a mile in your students' shoes. I grew up in a non-English-speaking family. My parents were from Mexico and my father was a farm worker. So I faced many of the challenges that your students now face, learning a second language and a second culture. The teasing on the bus, the ill-fitting clothes, the "funny-smelling" lunches—I remember it all too well. However, one kind teacher, Mrs. Elizabeth Pinkerton, made a big difference. She also inspired me to become a teacher myself.

Then as a young teacher, I walked a mile in your shoes. Teaching at one of the first Newcomer Schools, created to help California serve a sudden influx of non-English speakers, I was hired because I had a Bilingual Education teaching credential (Spanish/English specialist). But as I was unable to speak Hmong and the many other languages spoken by my students, my bilingual training was not extremely helpful.

In short order, I had nearly as many different languages in my class as students. Unable to communicate with my students and not knowing what to do for them, I hit rock bottom as a teacher. I was desperate to find some way to break through the language barrier. Many tears and several epiphanies later, I developed some useful strategies that I am going to share with you.

red. Red Faculty

Jo Gusman is a teacher, educational consultant, and author with more than 30 years of teaching experience and specialized training in bilingual and biliteracy education. She conducts seminars for teachers and administrators around the world and teaches courses in Literacy and Curriculum at California State University, Sacramento. Her work with English-language learners was featured on the NBC television series, "The New Kids In Town." She also has received presidential recognition and numerous awards for excellence in teaching. She is the founder and president of New Horizons in Education, Inc., a staff development organization which provides seminars.

How Is Language Acquired?

Think about where you do the most talking: When you're sharing a meaningful experience with family or friends? When you're fulfilling some role or responsibility? Well, cognitive psychologists and language-learning researchers have discovered that those factors are important for language acquisition to take place and for reading and writing skills to develop. The experts have determined that a comfortable, nonthreatening, and affirming learning environment is vital to students' success.

What Is the Process of Language Acquisition?

Most experts agree that students pass through five stages of language acquisition on their way to native-like fluency and reading and writing competence in English. Although the process is predictable, each individual develops at an individual rate and may exhibit characteristics of several stages simultaneously. In addition, this process is twofold. It takes place the first time with social language and then again with the language needed for content-area learning—academic language.

STAGES OF LANGUAGE ACQUISITION

Stage 1	Preproduction	This is called the silent period. At this stage, students are watching and taking in information about the new language, absorbing its sounds and patterns. They may understand a few words and respond nonverbally with gestures or drawings.
Stage 2	Early Production	At this stage, students listen with greater understanding. They can identify familiar people, places, objects. They might respond with one- or two-word phrases and recite or repeat some frequently used language. They may be able to follow along with simple, illustrated read-alouds.
Stage 3	Speech Emergence	At this stage, students begin to produce longer phrases and simple sentences, usually with many errors. They begin to try out new vocabulary to express original ideas. They may be able to do some independent reading with very simple text.
Stage 4	Intermediate Fluency	At this stage, students can read a greater range of texts independently, express basic ideas, offer explanations, and tell simple narratives. Vocabulary grows and mistakes begin to diminish. Students use some standard forms when writing. They can explore concepts in greater depth.
Stage 5	Advanced Fluency	At this stage, students will be able to understand, read, speak, and write the new language with close to the same fluency as native speakers of the same age.

BICS and CALPS

Have you ever heard a teacher say, "I have students who pretend not to understand English whenever we do any content-area work. But I hear them speaking English at lunchtime, so they're not fooling me?"

BICS Actually, there is a scientific explanation for this. According to Dr. James Cummins, a leading expert in literacy development, language learners typically acquire language that expresses basic human needs first (1994). The technical term is Basic Interpersonal Communication Skills (BICS). BICS stick. Think about a language you learned and have mostly forgotten. What words do you still remember? They're probably not content-area related.

CALPS Later in the process, students begin to use their new language to gain content-area concepts and knowledge. This is called Cognitive Academic Language Proficiency Skills (CALPS). At this point, the academic language needed for learning specific subjects is daunting enough to send students back to earlier stages in the language-learning process. They may need to begin again with a silent period of listening. Students must comprehend new concepts with new vocabulary and apply high-order thinking skills to unfamiliar genres and procedures.

Basic Interpersonal Communications Skills (BICS)

- Beginning listening and speaking skills
- Language addressing basic human needs
- Simple conversation structures and vocabulary
- Language appropriate to social settings

Cognitive Academic Language Proficiency Skills (CALPS)

- Content-area concepts and skills
- Language of literacy and formal writing
- Narrative and expository text structures
- Test-taking structures, procedures, and strategies

Reading and Writing Begin With Oral Language

English-language learners need to develop listening and speaking skills. Think of these skills as if they were money in the bank. With plenty of oral language in their accounts, students can make withdrawals for reading and writing. Without reserves of oral language to draw on, students decode sounds without meaning and are unable to transfer their skills to meaningful reading and writing. Here's an example: Imagine a student encountering the word *recipe.* It looks unfamiliar. But after remembering how his teacher used this word when they cooked in the classroom, and showed the students a recipe card, the student then tries sounding out the word and realizes, "Oh, I know this word! Recipe—something you use when cooking." Now imagine that the student has never heard the word *recipe.* That connection isn't made.

Listening and Speaking

Unsurprisingly, listening is the first literacy skill that a new English-language learner will attempt. This takes place during what is known as the silent period. Don't be alarmed by the silence. This is actually a period of active listening. In fact, if you rearrange the letters in the word *silent,* you get *listen!* During the silence, students listen to the rhythm and structure of the new language. They also "listen with their eyes"—internalizing the body language of the new language and culture. This is a very critical stage. Although beginning language-learners may not be able to decode for meaning, they are actively listening and looking for recognizable patterns and messages made understandable by the context. Dr. Stephen Krashen, a well-known second-language acquisition researcher, calls this "comprehensible input" (1985).

Using Comprehensible Input

Back when I was at the Newcomer School, I was trying to teach my students about condensation. I realized I wasn't getting through to them. One night, feeling particularly demoralized, I watched a TV show that I thought might cheer me up. It was a Charlie Brown cartoon special. Suddenly, there was my epiphany. Charlie Brown's teacher (like all the adults in the cartoon) sounded like this: *wah wah wah.* It was the first time I realized how I sounded to my English-language learners who did not understand social or academic English.

Armed with my new realization, I tried to give my students a break from my constant stream of unintelligible language by using pictures and media that offer nonverbal means of communication. I chose words that referred to familiar people, objects, and places and steered clear of abstract language. I saw a big difference in my students' comprehension. For English-language learners, remember the old cliché: a picture is worth a thousand words.

Here's another way to improve comprehensible input. It's a technique I call "The Language Signal." The signal is an exaggerated physical, verbal, and visual cue. A blend of all three is best. For example, you might loudly say, "Key point!" while holding a set of keys and jingling them. This helps students know where and when to apply their best active listening skills.

Also try the "Chunk and Chew" technique. Present information in a small "chunk" (under ten minutes) and then give students five to ten minutes of processing time to "chew" on it. That could be quiet thinking time, journal writing, or peer discussions. This gives English-language learners time to translate and rephrase information in a way that's familiar.

Lowering the Affective Filter

Producing language involves risk. You can fake listening somewhat with a well-placed nod. But you can't fake speaking. Some students may compensate by being overly cautious. They may tell you in perfect English that they can't speak English. The goal is to create an environment in which they won't be afraid to try. The key to this is what Dr. Krashen calls the "affective filter"(1985).

Have you ever had the feeling that your teaching was going "in one ear and out the other"? That may be a result of the affective filter. The affective filter is an emotional shield. When it's up, nothing gets through. All of the students' energy is spent protecting their feelings and self-esteem. Fear of failure, rejection, humiliation, and stress raise students' filters. The threat need only be perceived. When students feel safe, included, and calm, the filter comes down. When the filter is down, students can be receptive to the environment, you, and the skills and concepts you teach.

Run a quick affective filter check.

- Look at your classroom with new eyes. What kind of feeling does the room have? Is it warm and welcoming?

- Think about the social environment of the classroom. Are there ground rules that foster respect? Don't forget the power of modeling the appropriate behavior.

- Consider your body language. Linguistics research shows that about 80 percent of communication takes place on a nonverbal level. A smile needs no translation.

- Consider how much information is presented in English—orally and in written form. Is there any way to make this more comprehensible and, therefore, more welcoming?

Finally, try to resist the urge to correct students' grammar and pronunciation. In the beginning, it is more important for them to feel comfortable exploring and experimenting with the structures, patterns, and rhythm of the new language, than it is for them to get it perfectly right. They will seek editing or correction when they are ready for it. In the meantime, use a gentle correction technique called "Motherese." That means restating correctly what the student said without mentioning the mistake.

Strategies to Make Language Accessible

- Add images or media to information you present orally or in writing.

- Choose words that refer to familiar people, objects, and places.

- Use language signals so that students know when to apply their best active listening.

- Present new information in small chunks and give students thinking, writing, or discussion time to process it.

- Ensure that your classroom environment is safe and welcoming.

- Set ground rules that foster respect.

- When students make an error, answer or restate what they said using the correct form and without drawing attention to the error.

Reading and Writing

So many opportunities exist in your classroom to extend oral-language activities into reading and writing. Set up a print-rich environment that encourages meaningful reading and reference during reading and writing activities. For example, label parts of the classroom, or have students write classroom labels, and read the labels while conducting classroom "tours." Students can even read them back to you chorally. Use visuals to make environmental print more meaningful. For example, if you have a rotation schedule with "Computer Group," add a picture of a computer so that students visualize and connect meaning to the words.

Meaningful Discussion

Class discussions become meaningful reading and writing activities when you read and record them together. For example, after you generate word lists, sentences, or paragraphs with students, read them chorally or in an echo fashion. Do this by reading a word or chunked phrases aloud and instructing students to repeat after you. When you read, and while students are repeating, track the words with your finger to connect oral language and print. This strategy allows students to see models of proficient writing, hear examples of fluent reading, and participate confidently. In the early stages of language acquisition, students will be much more comfortable reading with their peers and following a model.

Reading Strategies

These reading strategies will draw students in and tap their prior knowledge.

- Guide students to read texts around a common topic. This way, they will come across the same words over and over again, making retention more likely.

- Before reading with English-language learners, use picture walks to introduce new vocabulary, activate prior knowledge, discuss real-life connections, and make predictions.

- Anticipate challenging words or concepts and provide role-playing or similar experiences to build meaning.

- Use repeated reading strategies, like partner reading and Readers' Theater, that expose students to the same text multiple times. The more time students have with a text, the more comfortable they will be reading it.

All of these strategies will help you support your students to confidently and successfully transition from speaking to reading and writing.

Writing to Build Comprehension

If students are hesitant to write, make the task more approachable.

- **Think aloud** as you model writing for your English-language learners.
- **Provide sentence frames** for students to fill in, or word cards that can be arranged.
- **Use graphic organizers** to encourage students to get their ideas down before writing.
- **Have students write** with a partner and provide references such as picture dictionaries.
- **Divide** the writing process into simple, manageable steps that are practiced many times.
- **Model** writing before expecting students to grasp features of different writing forms.
- **Provide** frequent opportunities for students to share within the classroom community.

The Benefits of Oral-Language Practice

The best way to practice oral-language is through a context that will be meaningful to students. Consider their important role as family translator, for example. Or tie the practice to a subject area being studied or read about in class. For example, tell students you want them to learn how to recognize spoken numbers so they can be successful in math class. Making oral-language practice relevant will help you reap the greatest benefits for developing their reading and writing skills.

Building Vocabulary

The research shows that it takes about ten usages in purposeful, meaningful contexts for a student to acquire a new vocabulary word. So oral-language practice is a good way to get new vocabulary to stick. Think about particular vocabulary sets your students need.

- Do they need to begin with classroom objects and simple classroom commands?
- Do they need survival English skills because they've been designated the family interpreter?
- Do they need help with idiomatic language?
- Are you doing content-area reading?

Use oral-language practice activities to support your students' specific needs. As their familiarity with the spoken form of the word increases, ensure that they have multiple opportunities to connect to reading and writing.

Phonemic Awareness

Before students can sound out words, they must be able to hear them. Not all of the sounds in English exist in other languages. The brain is wired to hear sounds of the first language. Don't get frustrated with students who can't seem to hear the difference between *pet* and *pat*. To them, these words sound the same. Meaningful oral-language practice can help them learn to make such distinctions.

Correct Grammatical Forms

Oral language practice is a good way to reinforce basic grammar points such as irregular verbs, third-person "s," or prepositions. However, for English-language learners these represent fine points that are difficult to master even at the advanced fluency stage. If you happen to know your students' language well enough, help make them conscious of the differences in syntax between their language and English. It's best to do this physically with sentence strips or some other manipulative. This way they will gain practice seeing these grammatical forms in writing.

Standards

Oral-language practice will directly benefit teachers who are required to meet state standards. The objectives outlined in state English-Language Arts and English-Language Development standards, as well as those identified by TESOL (Teaching English to Speakers of Other Languages) can also provide you with a helpful framework for meeting students' second-language needs.

Social Language

Students pick up social language quickly because it addresses their basic communication needs (remember BICS!). You can facilitate this process by giving students theme-based practice with the typical language used in particular situations such as greetings, apologies, words of encouragement or sympathy, etc. Also, get to know their interests and use them as language-learning contexts.

Culturally Appropriate Language

Some students may need explicit information about what is considered appropriate in this culture within a variety of settings, i.e., the basketball court, the theater, the principal's office, the school cafeteria. Using formal or informal language, avoiding sexist or racist language, maintaining comfortable personal distance, and rules for eye contact are some examples.

Academic Language

Academic language includes content-area specific concepts, skills, and vocabulary most commonly found in content-area reading and writing. It also includes the structures, formats, and processes of textbooks, informal assessment, and standardized tests.

Building Community

For students to acquire language, the classroom needs to offer cooperative learning activities and structures. One more advantage of oral-language practice is its interactive nature. Games and conversations can help encourage cooperative learning. These activities get students talking to others outside their usual social group. This creates a greater sense of inclusion and trust in the classroom.

Practical Ideas for Making Language Practice Successful

From my experience in the classroom and as a consultant to schools and school districts, I have learned that to create effective language acquisition programs, three elements need to be in place. They are: foundation, framework, and tools.

A Solid Foundation

Begin by examining the research about language acquisition and teaching.

- Do you know how language is best learned? If so, how will you provide a meaning-centered and culturally relevant context for learning?

- Examine your beliefs about your students. How well do you understand their cultures and languages?

- Are your students' cultures important to you? If so, how will you make your classroom culturally inclusive?

Examine your goals and devise concrete plans to meet them.

A Strong Framework

Research on effective teaching offers this simple framework for maximizing benefits for English-language learners.

Plan

- Identify the necessary concepts, skills, and vocabulary.

- Set a meaningful context: a video, a nature walk, guest speakers, foods, music, or photographs.

- Consider room arrangement, materials, books, and classroom resources.

Teach

- Build anticipation: play a song, bring in a surprise guest, be creative.
- Set a purpose for learning. Explain why students need to know the content you teach.
- Provide directions using multi-sensory techniques and limiting teacher talk.
- Check for understanding and model reflection-type thinking while reading or writing.
- Allow time for peer sharing, journal time, and clarification/confirmation requests or rereading.

Practice

- Demonstrate and model all parts of an oral reading or a writing activity that students will be asked to do.
- Check for understanding by having students restate the task.
- Assess students' performance. Does a skill need reteaching?
- Celebrate success. Encourage students in their efforts.

Research-Based Tools You Can Use

Once you have a framework, you need tools. In this book you'll find two community-building activities and 50 language-development activities. First, use the community-building activities to establish a safe environment and encourage students to speak with one another. Then, move on to the language-development activities that emphasize listening and speaking and their connection to building reading and writing skills.

 Further Reading

Look up these professional resources to learn more about language development.

- Cummins, J. (1994). "The Acquisition of English as a Second Language." In Spangenberg-Urbschat, K., and Pritchard, R. (Eds.), *Reading Instruction for ESL Students.* Delaware: International Reading Association.

- Helman, L. A. (2004). "Building on the Sound System of Spanish: Insights From the Alphabetic Spellings of English-Language Learners." *The Reading Teacher,* 57(5), 452–460.

- Kinsella, K. (1996). "Designing Group Work That Supports and Enhances Diverse Classroom Work Styles." *TESOL Journal,* 6(1), 24–30.

- Kinsella, K. (1994). "'What Is Cowboy?': Preparing English Learners for a Culturally Based Curriculum." *Ideas for Excellence,* 3(1), 1–3.

- Krashen, S. (1985). *Insights and Inquiries.* Hayward, CA: Alemany Press.

- Sarosy, P., and Sherak, K. (2002). "Empowering Students by Teaching the Language of the Classroom." *CATESOL Journal,* 14(1), 271–282.

Why Use Special Features?

READ 180 Software has support features that you can activate to help English-language learners:

- Understand Topic Software video content.
- Decode and recognize English sounds.
- Read along with a fluent model.
- Make connections between new vocabulary and words from their first language.
- Navigate within the Software.

Software Support for the English-Language Learner

Remember to activate the READ 180 Software support for English-language learners.

First-Language Support

The *READ 180* Topic Software includes features that are specifically designed for English-language learners to provide support in their first language. Use the step-by-step directions on the next page to activate these features in the *Scholastic Achievement Manager* (SAM).

- **Video Translation** Students will hear a short, one- or two-sentence preview of the video in their first language. This preview helps students understand the Topic Software video content.
- **Vocabulary Word Translation** Students hear translations of passage vocabulary words highlighted within Reading Zone passages. This translation of key words helps students make important connections between new vocabulary and words they know in their first language.

The **Video and Vocabulary Word Translations** are available in these languages:

- ✓ Cantonese
- ✓ Hmong
- ✓ Vietnamese
- ✓ Haitian Creole
- ✓ Spanish

- **Spanish Pronunciation Tips** Students hear explanations of commonly confused sounds and receive helpful pronunciation suggestions in Spanish. These pronunciation tips help Spanish-speaking students decode and recognize English sounds.

Additional Support for English-Language Learners

These additional Software features are designed for all learners, but provide further support for English-language learners. Use the step-by-step directions on the next page to activate these features in SAM.

- **Text Captioning** Students see and read along with captions for the video narration. Text captioning improves students' word recognition and understanding by enabling them to see and hear the language at the same time.
- **Button Rollover** Students see text labels and hear audio prompts when using Software buttons. When button rollover is activated, students hear the buttons' text label read aloud, helping them navigate within the Software.
- **Reading Speed** Students hear a Reading Zone passage read Word-by-Word or Phrase-by-Phrase at a speed, from 1 (slowest) to 5 (fastest), chosen by the teacher. The adjustable practice speed allows for progressive levels of reading support for English-language learners, depending on their need.

Universal Features

These Software features are available to all students, and support the reading progress of English-language learners. You do not have to activate these features.

- **Dictionary Screen** In Reading Zone passages, students hear a highlighted vocabulary word pronounced, broken into word parts, spelled, and defined. They can also receive a decoding tip. When English-language learners use these features on the dictionary screen, they associate a printed word with its pronunciation.
- **Audio Recordings** Students record and then listen to themselves read a passage. Audio recordings may be used easily to monitor the pronunciation, fluency, and phrasing of English-language learners.

All of these Software features support English-language learners' acquisition of English-language skills by offering systematic, individualized, and differentiated instruction in a respectful environment.

Accessing Special Software Features

To adjust and customize settings for English-language learners, follow these instructions:

How to Adjust Settings to Individualize Support

1 Go to the home page of SAM.

2 Click the **Roster** tab.

3 Double-click the student, group, or class name on the **SmartBar** to set options.

4 Click the **Manage** link next to the *READ 180* icon to open the **Program Settings** window.

5 Make your selections from the **English-Language Learner Options** and **Support Options** menus.

6 Click **Save** when you are finished making adjustments.

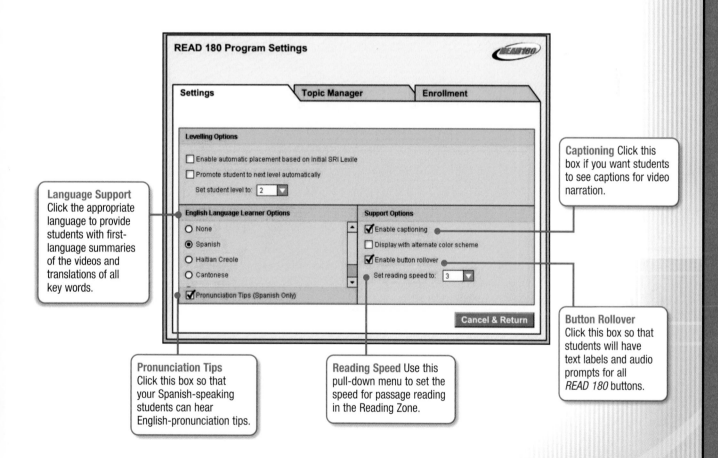

Language Support Click the appropriate language to provide students with first-language summaries of the videos and translations of all key words.

Captioning Click this box if you want students to see captions for video narration.

Button Rollover Click this box so that students will have text labels and audio prompts for all *READ 180* buttons.

Pronunciation Tips Click this box so that your Spanish-speaking students can hear English-pronunciation tips.

Reading Speed Use this pull-down menu to set the speed for passage reading in the Reading Zone.

Listening and
Speaking Activities

Lesson 1

Drag Your Mouse

Background Tell students that you are going to help them focus on recognizing and understanding different words that they will encounter as they use *READ 180* materials.

Demonstration Invite students to gather around a computer. Point to the screen as you say *screen*. Ask a volunteer to point to the screen while the whole class repeats the word. Repeat this with the *mouse* and a *disc* (or Topic Software).

Turn on the computer. Move the mouse to an icon and click. Say: *Click the icon* as you perform the action. Say: *Drag the file to the trash* as you drag an item to the trash icon. Say: *Shut down the computer* as you show students how to do this. Give examples of typical instructions students will hear in class, such as: *Click the Go On button,* and so on.

Repeat this process with the CD player. Point to the features and familiarize students with their names and their functions. (See Idea Bank.) Point out that some words have more than one meaning, such as *mouse* and *play*.

Activity Tell students that they are going to have an opportunity to create a dialogue between two students or a teacher and a student using the vocabulary they just reviewed.

1. Ask students to choose a partner.

2. Assign each pair three or four words from the Idea Bank.

3. Give students five minutes to work with their partners to prepare a role-playing dialogue that uses all or most of their words.

4. As students prepare their dialogues, offer assistance as necessary.

5. When students have finished, let partners take turns role-playing for the class.

IDEA BANK

screen	click	play
mouse	drag	login
microphone	shut down	fast forward
disc	headphones	password
	CD player	

Modifications Pair beginning English-language learners with more proficient English speakers who can support them in their role-playing.

STUDENT OBJECTIVES

- Listen for meaning.
- Practice classroom commands and language
- Develop technological vocabulary

TESOL Standards

- Academic Language
- Social Language

Additional Practice

Listening/Speaking
Challenge pairs of students to select another type of technology—for example, a cell phone, television, or DVD player —and tell how it is used.

Lesson 2

Memory Game

STUDENT OBJECTIVES

- Name everyday items
- Listen actively
- Practice and build vocabulary

TESOL Standards

- Academic Language
- Social Language
- Culturally Appropriate Language

Additional Practice

Speaking
Repeat the activity, this time choosing a student to remove the objects for classmates to identify.

Reading
Display cards with object names along the chalk ledge and have students match each item with its name. As a variation, have students sort cards by content area.

Background This activity provides an opportunity to build and practice vocabulary in varied content areas. You can use objects or pictures, depending on the theme. Begin with classroom objects that students come across in their everyday lives.

Demonstration Place items from the Idea Bank on a table. Hold them up one at a time and ask volunteers to name them. Repeat each word aloud and have the rest of the class say it with you. Provide language as necessary. Give students time to practice new or unfamiliar words.

Activity Play a game with students in which they must remember objects and name them.

1. Ask students to study the objects carefully and to try to remember each object on the table and what it is called.

2. Have students turn away or close their eyes while you remove an object.

3. Ask them to look at the objects remaining on the table and to tell what is missing.

4. Have students close their eyes again as you remove another object. Ask students to tell what object is missing.

Continue until all objects have been removed. Challenge students to recall all the objects. Place them on the table as students name them. Have students write the name of each object on a card.

IDEA BANK		
pencil	map	eraser
marker	scissors	pen
dictionary	stapler	paper clip
globe	pencil sharpener	chalk

Modifications Vary vocabulary and themes according to students' level of English. For students with greater English proficiency, use words such as *thesaurus, ruler, thermometer,* and *backpack.* Other themes may include: math-related items such as a *calculator, compass, ruler, textbook,* and so on.

Lesson 3

Talking About Books

Background Explain that books can be divided into two main types: fiction and nonfiction. Fiction books tell a story about characters and events that are not real. Nonfiction books deal with real people and events. Point out that nonfiction books often have features that help readers find things more easily.

Demonstration Display one fiction and one nonfiction book. Point to the title of the fiction book and say: *The title of this book is _____.* Ask a volunteer to point to the title of the nonfiction book and read it. Write *title* on sticky notes and stick them beside the title of each book. Repeat this with the author and chapter titles.

Hold up the nonfiction book. Open to the Table of Contents and point to it as you say *Table of Contents.* Explain that it lists the parts or contents of the book and tells the page on which they are found. Write *Table of Contents* on a sticky note and stick it to the page.

Continue with the other words in the Idea Bank. Have students say each word with you and, if possible, have them point to the corresponding section in a sample book.

Activity Invite students to explore books in a hands-on activity as they label and talk about different parts of books.

1. Have students form small groups. Give each group four to five *READ 180* Paperbacks of varied genres and some sticky notes.

2. Name one of the book features.

3. Then, groups should work together to find this feature in their books, write the feature name on sticky notes, and place them in the appropriate sections of each book.

4. Repeat this with other features from the Idea Bank.

5. When students have finished, let groups take turns using complete sentences to tell the class about their findings.

IDEA BANK

title	conclusion/afterword
author	bibliography
table of contents	subheading
index	introduction/foreword/preface
glossary	illustration/photograph/map
chapter title	bold type

Modifications If students require extra help, let them refer to the sticky note labels in the books that you used in the demonstration.

STUDENT OBJECTIVES

- Listen for meaning
- Describe parts of a book
- Use nonverbal communication

TESOL Standards

- Academic Language

Additional Practice

Listening/Speaking
Repeat this activity letting students take turns calling out feature names for others to identify.

Lesson 4

Feeling Fine

STUDENT OBJECTIVES

- Express feelings
- Recognize adjectives that describe feelings
- Use nonverbal communication to express emotion

TESOL Standards

- Social Language
- Culturally Appropriate Language

Additional Practice

Listening/Speaking
Introduce more complex feeling words such as *disappointed*, *furious*, and *lonely*. Have pairs of students use role-playing to act them out.

Background Explain that we use adjectives to describe people, places, and things. Adjectives can also describe the way a person is feeling, such as *happy*, *angry*, and *sick*. Ask students to name other adjectives that tell about feelings, and write their ideas on the board.

Demonstration Express one of the words in the Idea Bank: for example, *happy*. Make a big smile as you say: *I'm happy*. Have students repeat the word and facial expression with you. Repeat this with the other words in the Idea Bank and words students suggest.

Say one of the words aloud and ask students to make faces or actions to express it. Encourage them to be very expressive.

Activity Play a game with students in which they recognize facial expression and body language to convey the way a person is feeling. You will need a number of magazines with photos or newspaper comic strips featuring people with various expressions.

1. Distribute magazines or comic strips to each pair of students.

2. Have one student in each pair select two to three people or characters with different feelings. They should write a word describing each of the feelings (from the Idea Bank or other word) on an index card.

3. Have these students give the cards and photos/comics to their partners, who must then correctly match the photos/comics with the cards that describe the expressions in them.

Continue until all feeling words have been identified correctly.

IDEA BANK			
happy	angry	tired	confused
sad	scared	worried	proud

Modifications Challenge more proficient English speakers to describe feelings in a sentence that explains when or why someone might feel that way. To help less proficient English speakers, you may want to draw smiling and other expressive faces on the card.

Lesson 5
Command Performance

Background Explain that commands are statements that tell what to do. Point out that when playing a sport or in an emergency situation, it is fine to shout commands. At other times it is important to add the word *please*.

Demonstration Introduce the following command: *Please take out your pencils.* Pantomime the activity and write the command on the board.

Review the commands listed in the Idea Bank. Have students repeat the words as they perform each action with you. Use the word *please* each time. As students become familiar with the vocabulary, give commands, but do not perform the actions. See how many students can perform the actions without needing to follow your example.

Activity Invite students to practice giving commands to their classmates. Write the commands that you've reviewed during the demonstration on slips of paper. Toss them in a bag.

1. Choose a student to go first. Have this student draw a slip of paper and read the command for the other students to follow. Instruct students to listen for the word *please*.

2. If the student giving the command forgets to say *please*, have the others remind him or her by saying: *What do you say?*

3. Every time a student gives a command with the word *please* and the others are able to complete the action, remove the slip from the bag.

4. When students empty the bag of commands, ask them to think of additional commands.

IDEA BANK

Please raise your hand.
Please find a partner.
Please line up.
Please push in your chairs.
Please take your seats.
Please take out a piece of paper.
Please close your eyes.
Please open your books.
Please stand up.
Please write your name.
Please close your books.
Please pay attention.

Modifications For students with less English proficiency, you may want to use simpler vocabulary that refers to everyday actions: *brush your teeth, wash your hands, comb your hair,* etc. For more advanced students use a longer chain of commands.

STUDENT OBJECTIVES

- Understand commands
- Practice classroom terms
- Perform action words
- Use polite language
- Listen for meaning
- Follow directions

TESOL Standards
- Social Language
- Culturally Appropriate Language
- Academic Language

Additional Practice

Listening
Repeat the activity using commands that include prepositions. For example, *please put the pen on top of the desk; please slide your books under the desk; please stand in front of the board;* etc.

Lesson 6
Ten Questions

STUDENT OBJECTIVES

- Ask present-tense questions
- Give short answers
- Identify places in a city or community
- Understand how to read a map

TESOL Standards

- Social Language
- Culturally Appropriate Language

Additional Practice

Speaking
Repeat this activity using other notable features in the community, such as transportation hubs, bridges, or bodies of water.

Background Explain to students that knowing how to ask questions is an important skill that will allow them to acquire information about any subject. Tell students that they will be using questions to identify different places in their city or community.

Demonstration Display a map of your city or community. Let students take turns pointing to different places that appear on the map. These might include a library, post office, and police station. Write the names of the places on index cards.

Talk with students about each place and who works there. Then help them understand what kinds of things are done in each of these community places.

Display the cards along the chalk rail. Make a statement about one of the places, such as: *People go there to get books.* Have a volunteer point to the correct card and read the place name *(library).*

Activity Invite students to play a "Ten Questions" game in which they ask questions to help them identify a specific place in the community.

1. Divide the class into two teams.

2. Put the place name cards in a bag. Have Team 1 members take a card from the bag and read the place name to themselves.

3. Students on Team 2 should ask simple questions that can be answered with yes or no: for example, *Do firefighters work there? Do you get books there?*

4. Have Team 1 answer the questions.

5. Team 2 should guess the place in up to ten questions.

6. Continue the game, letting teams take turns asking and answering questions.

IDEA BANK

library	park	museum
post office	school	theater
police station	hospital	college
fire station	stadium	church

Modifications You may want to write cloze sentences on the board that less proficient English speakers can use to guide them when asking questions. These might include: *Do _____ work there? Do you _____ there?*

Lesson 7

Thirty, Thumbs, and Other Words With /th/

Background Certain sounds may be very challenging for English-language learners to distinguish. These sounds will vary according to the students' first language, but one difficult sound for many is /th/, as in *thumb.*

Demonstration Write one of the words from the Idea Bank on the board: for example, *think.*

Point to it and say *think,* /th/, *think.* Have students repeat the sound and word with you. Tell students to place their tongues between their upper and lower teeth and force air between them to make the /th/ sound. To check that they are pronouncing /th/ correctly, have students hold an index finger to their mouths as if gesturing someone to be quiet. Say /th/. The tongue should stick out far enough to touch the finger.

Have students pronounce the other words, making sure that they pronounce /th/ correctly. Then ask volunteers to go to the board, say a word, and underline the letters that stand for the /th/ sound.

Activity Invite students to play a game to see how many times they hear the /th/ sound.

1. Have students line up across the classroom, facing front. They should be at least ten steps from where you are standing.

2. Slowly and clearly, say words with and without the /th/ sound.

3. Tell students that when they hear a word with the /th/ sound, they should take one giant step forward.

4. Students who step forward when the spoken word did not have the /th/ sound should take two giant steps back.

5. Repeat this until one student reaches you.

IDEA BANK

think	thumb	bath	teeth
thing	thirty	birth	mouth
thin	thirteen	cloth	north
thick	thought	math	south

Modifications Use the following words to challenge more proficient English speakers: *thermometer, thermal, thermos, thimble, thicket, thigh, thief.*

STUDENT OBJECTIVES

- Identify digraphs
- Listen for sound recognition
- Pronounce /th/

TESOL Standards

- Academic Language

Additional Practice

Listening/Speaking
Repeat this game using the sounds that students are studying in their phonics lessons.

Reading
For practice reading words with /th/, write the words from the Idea Bank on the board. Say each word in random order or give clues for the students to use to identify the words. Have students point to each word and read it aloud.

Phonics
1 **RDI Book 1:** Digraphs

Lesson 8

Same Story

STUDENT OBJECTIVES

- Use synonyms
- Retell a story
- Complete a cloze paragraph

TESOL Standards

- Academic Language
- Social Language

Additional Practice

Speaking
For additional practice using synonyms, divide the class into two groups. Say a word and have groups take turns naming the synonym.

Synonyms

1 **RDI Book 1:** Synonyms

Background Explain that a synonym is a word that has the same or almost the same meaning as another word, so the two words can be used interchangeably. Tell students that they can use synonyms to replace "tired words" (overused or dull words) to make stories or conversations more interesting.

Demonstration Write the following anecdote on a sheet of chart paper:

> I had a <u>good</u> visit with my aunt. We had a <u>fun</u> time. The food was <u>good</u>. The weather was <u>good</u>, so we went to the beach. It was <u>fun</u>.

Read the anecdote aloud. Tell students that the underlined words are "tired words." Select one of the words: for example, *good*. Challenge students to brainstorm a list of synonyms that could replace the first use of *good*. (See the Idea Bank.) Do the same for *fun*. List all the ideas on the board. Have students read the words.

Activity Invite students to use synonyms to make new versions of the anecdote. You will need to make a handout of the story, leaving blanks in place of the underlined words.

1. Have students choose a partner and give each pair a copy of the cloze passage.

2. Have partners work together to come up with words to write in each blank. They may refer to the list on the board or come up with their own ideas.

3. When they are done, each partner should read the story to the other.

4. Have sets of partners get together to share and compare responses, reading their versions aloud.

5. Point out how many different versions of the same dialogue students can make by using synonyms.

IDEA BANK

Synonyms for *good: excellent, fine, pleasant, lovely, agreeable, great*

Synonyms for *fun: enjoyable, amusing, entertaining, pleasurable, exciting*

Modifications Pair less proficient English speakers with more proficient ones who will be able to support them in this activity.

Lesson 9

Blue Jeans and Red Socks

Background Students will benefit from being able to describe not only what someone looks like, but what he or she is wearing. Teach or review the different articles of clothing that students wear and have them identify who among them is wearing these items.

Demonstration Say: *I see a red sweatshirt. Stand up if you are wearing a red sweatshirt.* Point to the student standing and ask the class: *What is he/she wearing?* Help them answer, *a red sweatshirt.* Repeat this with other articles of clothing from the Idea Bank. Modify the colors and articles of clothing in the Idea Bank to correspond with the clothing worn by students in your classroom.

Activity Tell students that you are going to describe what a person in the room is wearing. Add that you would like students to guess who the person is according to your description.

1. Look around the room and choose a student.

2. Describe what a person is wearing: for example, *He is wearing blue jeans and a red sweatshirt. He has on brown shoes and green socks.*

3. Give students time to look around and decide whom you are describing.

4. Have students raise their hands to offer guesses.

5. Repeat this activity, describing other people in different clothing.

IDEA BANK

Articles of clothing: sweatshirt, sneakers, sweater, shirt, jeans, jacket, socks, hat, shoes, purse

Colors: (in addition to red, blue, yellow, green, and orange) aqua, beige, tan, khaki, turquoise, maroon, fuchsia, mustard

---

Modifications To support less proficient English speakers, point to different articles of clothing as you describe what each person is wearing.

STUDENT OBJECTIVES

- Listen for meaning
- Follow directions
- Identify articles of clothing

TESOL Standards

- Social Language
- Culturally Appropriate Language

Additional Practice

Listening/Speaking
Let students take turns describing what someone is wearing while their classmates try to guess who is being described.

Reading/Writing
Bring in clothing ads for students to share. Help them find the words from the Idea Bank in the ads. Have pairs work together to write their own ads. Then have them exchange their ads with other pairs and identify colors and articles of clothing by name.

(Lesson 10)

Number Bingo

STUDENT OBJECTIVES

- Recognize numbers
- Listen for information

TESOL Standards

- Academic Language
- Social Language

Additional Practice

Listening/Speaking
Have students play the game again using another concept from the Idea Bank.

Background Bingo is a good way for students to practice saying and recognizing numbers. Use whatever numbers are most appropriate for the English and math levels of your students.

Demonstration To prepare for the demonstration, write the following numbers on index cards: 1 through 10, 12, 23, 34, 59, 78, 87, 127, 244, 351, 496, 567, 678, 892, 933, and 1000. Hold up the cards 1 through 10 one at a time and have volunteers say each number aloud. Then shuffle all the cards together and hold them up at random. Have volunteers say the numbers as you hold them up.

Shuffle the cards again and display them face up on a table. Say a number and ask a student to find the card and hold it up. The class should clap if the student holds up the correct number.

Activity Invite students to play a game of bingo to provide them with more practice saying and recognizing numbers.

1. Make a bingo board five squares by five squares and leave the squares blank. Make copies so that each student can have his or her own, and distribute them to the class.

2. Name each of the numbers on the number cards and have students write them in a square on their bingo boards.

3. Place the number cards in a bag. When students have completed their bingo boards, choose a volunteer to pick the numbers from the bag and read them aloud.

4. Students should find the number on their cards and cover it with a marker.

5. The first student to cover five numbers in a vertical, horizontal, or diagonal row is the winner. Have him or her read the numbers aloud and check them against the number cards.

IDEA BANK

random numbers in the 1,000s and 10,000s
fractions
decimals
percentages

Modifications Beginning English speakers will recognize the larger numbers but may find it difficult to name them. If a beginning speaker wins the game, allow him or her to write the numbers on the board. When they are all written, read them aloud and have the student point to them.

Lesson 11

Word Jumbles

Background This activity will give students an opportunity to listen to and recognize the letters of the alphabet. It will also provide them with good practice visualizing words and their spellings.

Demonstration Draw a large word web on a sheet of chart paper or on the board. Write *sports* in the center of the web. Ask volunteers to name sports and then write them on the web.

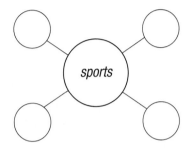

Choose one of the words that students suggest: for example, *baseball*. Write each letter of the word on an index card. Shuffle the cards and stand them up along the chalk ledge. Ask a volunteer to come to the front of the room and unscramble the letters to spell the name of a sport. Have the student read the word aloud.

Activity Group students into pairs and invite them to unscramble letters to spell the names of different sports.

1. Have pairs take out a sheet of paper and a pencil.

2. Scramble the letters of one of the sports words. Then dictate the scrambled letters.

3. Have students listen and write down the scrambled letters. Then challenge pairs to unscramble the letters to identify the word.

4. Students should raise their hands when they are done. Choose a volunteer to read the word.

Repeat this with all the words in the Idea Bank as well as other sports names that students suggested.

IDEA BANK

baseball	bicycling	ice hockey
basketball	swimming	football
soccer	running	skating

Modifications Extend the word web by writing related sports words around each sport. Support beginning English speakers by allowing them to refer to the word web while they do the activity.

STUDENT OBJECTIVES

- Recognize and write letters of the alphabet
- Listen attentively

TESOL Standards
- Academic Language
- Social Language

Additional Practice

Listening
Have students repeat this activity using a theme of their choice, or another theme that supports what they are learning in class.

Lesson 12

What's the Scoop?

STUDENT OBJECTIVES

- Ask and answer questions
- Discuss likes and dislikes
- Speak clearly
- Use interviewing skills

TESOL Standards

- Social Language
- Culturally Appropriate Language

Additional Practice

Listening/Speaking
Repeat this activity by having students interview each other using the questions in the Idea Box. They may extend the activity by interviewing family members at home.

Writing
Have students write a list of questions. Then have them trade papers with a partner who will write answers.

Background Interviewing is a good way to get students to talk about themselves and to learn about others. Tell students that an interviewer must always ask questions clearly and listen carefully and respectfully to the answer.

Demonstration Write the following list of questions on the board:

- *What kind of music do you like to listen to?*
- *What do you like to eat for dinner?*
- *What do you like to do in school?*
- *What do you like to do for fun?*
- *What do you like to do with your friends?*

Review the questions to make sure students understand all the words. Then ask a few students the first question. Let students take turns answering, beginning with the phrase: *I like to _____*. Repeat this with other questions.

Activity Have students interview each other to find out about their likes. Remind students that interviews are not about making judgements.

1. Have students choose partners.

2. One student is the interviewer; the other is the person being interviewed.

3. Tell the interviewer to ask his or her partner questions about what he or she likes.

4. The partner should try to answer all questions with complete sentences.

5. When the interview is over, partners may change roles.

IDEA BANK

What is your favorite sport?
What is your favorite food?
What is your favorite subject in school?
What is your favorite movie?
What is your favorite outdoor activity?

Modifications Beginning English speakers may answer the questions with one or two words; do not expect all students to answer in full sentences. Have more proficient students name more than one thing that they like in response to each question.

Lesson 13

Rhyme Scheme

Background Explain that rhyming words are words that share the same ending sounds: for example, *say* and *day*. Say each word slowly, being careful to pronounce it clearly. Help students hear the rhyme. Ask students to think of rhyming words in their first languages, and give them an opportunity to read the words.

Demonstration Choose one of the word groups in the Idea Bank: for example, *man, ban, can, pan,* and *ran.* Write *man* on the board.

Write *an* on one index card and *m* on another. Place the *m* card in front of the *an* card to make the word *man.* Have students say the word with you. Remove the *m* and replace it with a *b* card to make the word *ban.* Have students say the word. If students are not familiar with this word, explain what it means. Write *ban* under *man* on the board.

Continue replacing the *m* in *man* with other consonants in the alphabet. Have students read the groupings and guide them to identify which ones are words. List the words under *man* on the board. Repeat this with other word groups in the Idea Bank.

Activity This activity provides students with an opportunity to practice identifying rhyming words. You will need to choose a song and prepare the lyrics for students with the second word in rhyme pairs replaced with a blank. (Many song lyrics are available on the Internet.)

1. Divide the class into small groups.

2. Have the small groups work together to write the appropriate rhyming words in the blanks.

3. Verify correct rhymes and compare them to the actual lyrics. If possible, play the song for students.

IDEA BANK

man	hat	tin	log	met
ban	cat	fin	hog	set
can	rat	bin	fog	let
pan	sat	pin	bog	get
ran	bat	win	dog	yet

Modifications Choose a song that is appropriate for the age and English proficiency of your students. For younger and/or less proficient English speakers, you may want to use a very basic song and provide them with a list of the rhymed words in the song. For more proficient or older students, you may want to choose a popular song with more complex lyrics.

STUDENT OBJECTIVES

- Use accurate pronunciation
- Listen for rhyme
- Identify rhyming words

TESOL Standards

- Academic Language
- Social Language

Additional Practice

Reading/Writing
Ask pairs of students to brainstorm words that rhyme with a list of short words such as *jam, map, pen,* etc. Then have students write a short rhyme using at least two of these words.

Phonics

1 RDI Book 1: Short Vowels

Lesson 14

Pleased to Meet You

STUDENT OBJECTIVES

- Make introductions
- Use Mr., Mrs., and Ms.
- Role-play
- Express social courtesies

TESOL Standards

- Social Language
- Culturally Appropriate Language

Additional Practice

Listening/Speaking
Have students use the dialogue in the Idea Box to practice informal dialogue.

Background Explain that it is important to know the proper language to use in specific social situations. Tell students that they are going to learn how to introduce themselves to others and what to say when other people introduce themselves to them.

Demonstration Write the following dialogue on the board:

Luis:	*Hi, Eric. I'd like you to meet my mother.*
Mrs. Diaz:	*Hello, Eric. I'm Mrs. Diaz. It's a pleasure to meet you.*
Eric:	*It's nice to meet you, too, Mrs. Diaz.*

Read each line of dialogue and be sure students understand what is being said and who is saying it. Then ask students to echo-read the dialogue with you, focusing on intonation and pronunciation.

Have students repeat the dialogue substituting *father* and *Mr. Diaz* for *mother* and *Mrs. Diaz.* Write *Mrs.* and *Mr.* on the board. Point to each abbreviation and say it aloud. Have students repeat after you. Then write *Ms.* on the board, say it, and have students repeat. Explain the meaning of *Ms.* This may be an unfamiliar concept for many second-language learners.

Activity Invite students to create their own scenarios. Encourage them to substitute their own names for those in the dialogue.

1. Divide students into groups of three. Have them substitute *mother* or *father,* depending on the student playing the role.

2. Give groups time to practice the dialogue, focusing on correct pronunciation and appropriate intonation and expression.

3. Walk around the room as students practice, and model sentences when necessary.

IDEA BANK

Luis: Hi. My name is Luis and this is my sister Alicia.
Eric: Hi, Luis. Hi, Alicia. I'm Eric.
Luis and Alicia: Pleased to meet you.

Modifications Make mixed groups of beginning and proficient English speakers who can support each other as they role-play. More proficient English speakers can expand on the dialogues or extend the conversations.

Lesson 15

At the Market

Background Tell students that a word web is a graphic organizer that may be used to show how different words relate to a specific topic.

Demonstration Draw a word web on the board and write *hamburger* in the center. Ask students to brainstorm things that they could buy at a market to help make it. Write all of their suggestions on spokes around the center circle.

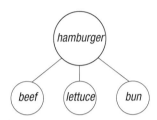

Use pictures to give students ideas about other things they can use in the recipe. Make another web with ingredients for french fries *(potatoes, oil, salt)*.

Activity Tell students that they are going to play a game in which they will need to listen to what classmates say, and remember and repeat the words. You will need an item found at a market, such as a potato.

1. Ask students to sit with you in a circle. Explain that they will be "shopping" for additional ingredients for their meal. Begin by saying: *I went to the market and I bought a potato.*

2. Pass a potato to the student sitting beside you and have him or her repeat your sentence and add to it: *I went to the market and I bought a potato and (oil).* Then that student should pass the potato to the next student.

3. Upon receiving the potato, each student should repeat what was bought before and add his or her own item. They may improvise by including drinks, napkins, and desserts.

Continue the game until all students have had a turn naming something that they bought or until they run out of things to name.

> **IDEA BANK**
>
> **at the beach ("I brought a _____.")**
> **on a camping trip ("I brought a _____.")**
> **at a restaurant ("I ordered _____.")**

Modifications You may want to write on the board a list of items named to help students remember what was previously said.

STUDENT OBJECTIVES

- Build vocabulary
- Categorize words
- Speak at an appropriate rate and volume

TESOL Standards

- Social Language
- Culturally Appropriate Language

Additional Practice

Listening/Speaking
Repeat this game using one of the themes suggested in the Idea Bank.

Writing/Reading
Have students write a shopping list of five food items and share the list with a partner. Ask students to include at least one food from their country of origin in their list and describe it.

Three Cheers!

STUDENT OBJECTIVES

- Recognize rhythm
- Use tone appropriate to purpose

TESOL Standards

- Social Language
- Culturally Appropriate Language

Additional Practice

Reading
Repeat this activity using poems that students have read in class or their favorite songs. Have them identify rhyming words as well.

Background Explain to students that people shout cheers during team games to encourage their team to win. Tell them that cheers generally have a specific rhythm and often use rhyming words. Ask students to share any cheers they know.

Demonstration Write the following cheer on a sheet of chart paper, or distribute it to the class in a handout.

1, 2, 3, 4,

Our team is going to score!

Read the cheer aloud and have students echo-read it with you several times. Then ask students to clap to the rhythm of the cheer. They should stress the beats on *2, 4, team,* and *score.* If not, clap with them and model the rhythm. Read through the other cheers in the Idea Bank and make sure students are familiar with the meanings.

Activity Tell students that they are going to explore the cheers' rhythms and clap them out.

1. Write a cheer from the Idea Bank on the board and read it aloud.

2. Clap on the accented syllables.

3. Ask students to read the cheer aloud and clap with you. Repeat this several times.

4. Encourage students to listen to the intonation and to hear the accented syllables.

5. Then say the cheer again but do not clap. Challenge students to hear the rhythm and to clap it out themselves. Repeat with the other cheers from the Idea Bank.

IDEA BANK

2, 4, 6, 8,
Our team is really great!
1, 3, 5, 9,
Our team's looking mighty fine!
5, 10, 15, 20,
Our team's gonna win by plenty!

Modifications You may want to write accent marks over the accented syllables to help students clap out the rhythm. Invite students who know other cheers to teach them to their classmates.

Lesson 17

Teens and Tens

Background Explain that there are many words that sound alike and therefore present both English speakers and English-language learners with some difficulties. Among words that sound alike and often cause confusion are the teens and tens, such as *fifteen* and *fifty*.

Demonstration Write the numbers *13* and *30* on the board. Then write each on an index card. Pronounce each number as you point to it. Have the class point and repeat with you. Hold one card in each hand. Say one of the numbers and have students point to the number you said.

Repeat this with the other numbers in the Idea Bank.

Activity Invite students to play a game in which they practice distinguishing the sounds of different numbers.

1. Divide students into two groups.

2. Give each group a set of number cards and have them place the cards face up on a table where everyone in the group can see them.

3. Say a number aloud and ask each group to hold up the card with the number you named.

4. The first group to hold up the correct card gets a point. Continue playing the game until one group gets 10 points.

5. Repeat the activity with students saying the numbers aloud to a partner to focus on clear speaking.

IDEA BANK

13, 30	14, 40	15, 50	16, 60
17, 70	18, 80	19, 90	

Modifications Form groups with mixed English proficiencies so that students can support each other in this activity.

STUDENT OBJECTIVES

- Listen actively and attentively
- Use accurate pronunciation
- Recognize numbers

TESOL Standards

- Academic Language
- Social Language

Additional Practice

Listening/Speaking
Repeat this activity with other words that sound similar and that students may confuse, such as *pen/pan/pin*, *ask(s)/ax*, *thin/thing*, *thing/think*, etc.

Lesson 18

Guess Who?

STUDENT OBJECTIVES

- Describe people
- Use adjectives
- Listen for meaning

TESOL Standards

- Social Language
- Culturally Appropriate Language

Additional Practice

Listening/Speaking

Write the names of music and film stars that students know on index cards or use their photos. Place them in a bag. Have students take turns picking a card or picture and describing the person for classmates to guess.

Background Remind students that adjectives are words that tell us more about someone or something. Tell students that they are going to learn adjectives they can use to describe one another.

Demonstration Write the following words on the board and review their meanings with students. Point to a student with curly hair and say: *He has curly hair.* Repeat this with other students and features.

Height	Hair Type	Hair Length	Eye Color	Hair Color
tall, short, medium	curly, wavy, straight, frizzy	long, short, medium	blue, green, brown	red, blond, brown, black

Use these adjectives to describe one of the students. Have students guess whom you are describing.

Activity Invite students to play a game using adjectives to help them describe classmates.

1. Have students choose a partner and write five adjectives that describe their partner on an index card. Be sure they write their partner's name above the description.

2. When students have finished, collect the cards and place them in a bag.

3. Choose a volunteer to pick a card from the bag and read the description aloud.

4. Classmates should use the description to identify the student being described. The first one to guess correctly can pick the next card.

Continue playing until students have identified all their classmates. (Note: This game can also be played by matching magazine photos to students' descriptions of them.)

IDEA BANK

height: tall, short, medium height
hair color: red hair, blond hair, brown hair, black hair
eye color: blue eyes, green eyes, brown eyes
hair type: curly hair, wavy hair, straight hair, frizzy hair
hair length: long hair, short hair, medium-length hair

Modifications For more proficient students, you may prefer to use more complex language.

Lesson 19
Guess What?

Background Explain that adjectives are words that describe things. Tell students that they are going to play a game in which they ask questions using adjectives to help them identify an object in the classroom.

Demonstration Point to a large object and say: *The _____ is big.* Point to a small object and say: *The _____ is small.* Review the words in the Idea Bank by choosing different objects in the classroom and using your hands to show their size, pointing to their color, or running your hand over them to show their texture.

Display a classroom object on your desk: for example, a globe. Use the adjectives in the Idea Bank to describe the globe.

> **It's medium-sized. It's round. It's smooth.**
> **It has many colors. It's metal.**

Point to a piece of chalk and say: *It is small.* Choose a volunteer to describe the color: for example, *It is white.*

Activity Tell students that you are going to think of an object in the classroom and they are to ask questions to help them determine the object you are thinking of.

1. Tell the class that they get only five chances to guess the object. Individual students get only one guess.

2. Have volunteers ask questions such as: *Is it blue?* Students should raise their hands and wait to be called on before asking their questions.

3. When a student thinks that he or she can identify the object, have the student whisper in your ear what the object is. The first student to guess correctly may select the next object.

4. If students guess incorrectly, show them the object and have them take turns using adjectives to describe it. Then choose another object and repeat the game.

IDEA BANK

Size: big, small, medium
Shape: round, square, triangular, flat
Color: red, yellow, blue, green, etc.
Texture: hard, soft, rough, smooth
Materials: plastic, metal, wood, cloth, paper

Modifications For students with less English proficiency, you may want to limit the lesson to words that describe size, shape, and color.

STUDENT OBJECTIVES

- Ask questions
- Use adjectives
- Describe characteristics of objects

TESOL Standards

- Social Language
- Culturally Appropriate Language

Additional Practice

Listening/Speaking
Let students take turns choosing an object and using adjectives to describe it. Classmates can guess what the object is.

Using Descriptive Words
2 **RDI Book 2:** Adjectives

Lesson 20

Animal Chains

STUDENT OBJECTIVES

- Identify initial and ending sounds of words
- Listen attentively
- Speak clearly
- Identify animals

TESOL Standards

- Social Language
- Academic Language

Additional Practice

Listening/Speaking
Repeat this activity with another theme from the Idea Bank.

Background Explain to students that this exercise will focus on identifying the first and last letters and sounds of words. At the same time, it will help them expand their vocabulary around given themes.

Demonstration Pick a subject from the Idea Bank, such as animals. Ask students to name as many animals as they can. Write the animal names on index cards and place them face up on a table.

Place one of the cards along the chalk ledge. Explain that word chains are chains of words that begin with the letter that the word before it ended with: for example, *tiger*, *rabbit, turtle.* Choose a card and have a volunteer name the last letter in the word. The student should then find another card that begins with that letter and place it next to the first card. Have students continue identifying letters and placing words according to this pattern. Add additional animal names on cards as necessary.

Activity Play a word-chain game with students. You will need a beanbag or another object for students to pass.

1. Invite students to sit in a circle.

2. Name an animal, for example, *tiger,* and pass the beanbag to the next student in the circle.

3. That student should think of an animal that begins with the letter *r* and say it: *rabbit,* for example.

4. Encourage students to say the words clearly so that the next student can hear the final letter.

5. Then that student passes the beanbag to the next student who continues the word chain.

Continue the game until students run out of animals.

IDEA BANK

animals	place names	people's names
foods	activities	

Modifications By leaving the display of animal cards along the chalk ledge, you will provide less proficient students with a model that they can refer to as they play the game.

Echo With a Twist

Background Explain that a contraction is two words combined together to make one. An apostrophe takes the place of the missing letters. Make sure that students understand that contractions are used in speaking and informal writing, not in formal writing.

Demonstration Write the following sentence on the board:

I'm reading a great book.

Read the sentence aloud, and have students repeat it. Then write and say: *I am reading a great book.* Point out that the first sentence uses a contraction, replacing the *a* with an apostrophe. Review the other contractions in the Idea Bank, identifying which letters are dropped.

Activity Invite students to play a game in which they practice using contractions.

1. Make a statement or ask a question, using either a contraction or the two words that the contraction would replace.

2. Tell students that they should echo exactly what you say, except that if you use a contraction, they should repeat the sentence using the two full words; and if you use the two words, they should repeat the sentence with a contraction.

3. Repeat, using sentences from the Idea Bank.

Alternate between saying the contractions and saying the two words. Extend the activity by using written statements or questions instead of oral ones.

IDEA BANK

I'm	I am	I'm/I am enjoying my book.
he's	he is	He's/He is on the soccer team.
you'll	you will	You'll/You will like this movie.
they're	they are	They're/They are going to the museum.
who's	who is	Who's/Who is going to babysit for my sister?
aren't	are not	We aren't/are not kidding.
didn't	did not	You didn't/did not tell me she is coming.
we've	we have	Did you hear we've/we have moved?

Modifications Challenge more proficient students to make contractions with other verbs and *not,* and to use them in sentences.

STUDENT OBJECTIVES

• Form contractions

• Listen attentively

TESOL Standards

• Academic Language

• Social Language

Additional Practice

Listening/Speaking
Repeat this activity with different contractions.

Reading/Writing
Write the contractions from the Idea Bank on the board. Add *can't* to the list and explain that it is the contraction of *cannot*. Have students work in pairs to write a note using words from the list to explain why they can't attend a school or family event.

Contractions

1 RDI Book 1: Contractions

Lesson 22

Getting From Here to There

STUDENT OBJECTIVES

- Follow directions
- Understand spoken directions

TESOL Standards

- Social Language
- Culturally Appropriate Language

Additional Practice

Listening/Speaking
Repeat this activity, letting students take turns giving the directions for others to follow.

Reading a Map
1 RDI Book 1: Read Maps

Background Knowing how to ask for and give directions is an important skill that students can learn to help them get around. Tell students that they are going to learn some new vocabulary that they can use to help them follow directions.

Demonstration Use masking tape to create three intersecting streets on the classroom floor. Stand on the corner of two streets and tell students that you are on the corner. Model crossing the street as you say: *Cross the street.* Model walking to the end of the block as you say: *Go to the end of the block.* If there is not enough space, draw the streets on the board and ask students to follow the directions with their fingers. Continue modeling the words in the Idea Bank as you say them.

Choose volunteers to stand up beside their desks and act out the directions that you say: for example, *Cross the street.* Make sure students understand the importance of looking both ways before they cross the street. Have the student model looking both ways and then crossing the street. Repeat this with other students and directions.

Activity Tell students that they will all have an opportunity to listen to and follow directions.

1. Point to a starting point on the taped streets and ask a pair of students to stand there.

2. Give directions from the Idea Bank for the pair to follow. Allow them to confer to confirm meaning.

3. If the pair follows the directions correctly, classmates can clap their hands to show their agreement. It not, model helpful behavior by saying *Let me show you the way,* and accompany the students to the right spot.

4. Give each pair several directions to follow.

IDEA BANK		
turn right	go (two) blocks	go to the end of the block
turn left	stop at the corner	cross the street

Modifications You may want to pair beginning English speakers with more proficient students who will help them interpret the directions and move accordingly along the roads.

Lesson 23

Bragging Rights

Background Explain to students that comparatives are words that compare items. In comparing two objects, *-er* is added to an adjective. In comparing more than two objects, *-est* is added to an adjective. If the adjective ends in *-y,* change the *y* to *i,* and then add *-er* or *-est.* Also, explain that some words, such as *good,* have irregular comparative forms, such as *good, better, best.*

Demonstration Choose one of the word groups from the Idea Bank: for example, *big/bigger/biggest.* Write it on the board and have students read it with you. Explain that *big* tells the size of one thing. When we want to compare two things, we use the comparative *bigger* to tell which item is the bigger of the two. For example, in the case of dogs: *A Dalmatian is bigger than a Chihuahua.* When we want to compare more than two things, we use the comparative *biggest: Of all kinds of dogs, the Irish wolfhound is the biggest.*

Write the word *pretty* on the board. Tell students that they must change the *y* to *i* and then add *-er* to make the word *prettier.* Help students use the word in a sentence: for example, *The pink flower is prettier than the yellow one.* Ask students to name other words that end in *-y (happy, funny).* Write them on the board and have volunteers write the comparative forms and read each one aloud.

Activity Explain the definition of *bragging.* Invite students to play a bragging game that will provide practice using comparatives.

1. Ask students to form two groups.

2. Ask one group to come up with a brag, such as: *We are smart* or *We get good grades.*

3. The other group should then answer using the correct comparative form, saying *We are smarter* or *We get better grades.*

4. Have the original group use the *-est* form, such as: *We are smartest* or *We get the best grades.*

5. Repeat, alternating which group goes first, providing adjectives from the Idea Bank as starting points.

STUDENT OBJECTIVES

- Use comparative and superlative forms
- Listen for meaning
- Describe objects and people
- Give information

TESOL Standards
- Academic Language
- Social Language
- Culturally Appropriate Language

Additional Practice

Writing
Have pairs of students choose two popular athletes, singers, comedians, or actors. Have each pair write a few sentences comparing the two famous people.

IDEA BANK

big	bigger	biggest
strong	stronger	strongest
fast	faster	fastest
funny	funnier	funniest
tall	taller	tallest
great	greater	greatest

Modifications For less proficient English speakers, create sentence strips they can use as a model when making their comparative statements: _____ *is bigger than*_____, and _____ *is the biggest of all.*

Scheduling Time

STUDENT OBJECTIVES

- Name the days of the week
- Name the months of the year
- Say numbers 1–31
- Follow directions

TESOL Standards

- Academic Language
- Social Language
- Culturally Appropriate Language

Additional Practice

Speaking

Ask students to brainstorm various classroom activities or special events. Write their suggestions on the board. Divide students into two groups. Each student should name one activity and a day they would like to do the activity, Record this information on the calendar. Each group will end up with a classroom planner.

Background Show students a calendar and explain that people use calendars to keep track of dates and events. Ask students to name some things that they might include on a calendar, such as birthdays, holidays, and school events.

Demonstration Make a photocopy of a monthly calendar page and give it to students. Have students point to the days of the week as you say them aloud. Then have them repeat them with you. Ask questions such as: *What day comes after Sunday?* or *What day comes before Thursday?* to provide students with additional practice naming the days of the week. Review all vocabulary in the Idea Bank and any other words, making reference to the calendar as necessary.

Activity Tell students that they are going to work together to schedule appointments on their calendars. Prepare copies of a monthly calendar so that various days are blacked out. Make several different versions so that each calendar has only a few free days in common. Tell students that on the crossed-out days they have plans and are not available.

1. Distribute the calendars.

2. Invent three occasions for which students need to get together—it could be for a dance, a team practice, and a study session.

3. Have students talk to their classmates and find a day on which at least three of them can make it.

4. Encourage them to speak politely and to use complete sentences.

IDEA BANK

Days of the week
Months of the year
Numbers 1–31
Sample phrases:
    Are you free on (Tuesday or the 13th)?
    I'm sorry. I'm not available that day.

Modifications Write down useful phrases and vocabulary on the board to which less proficient English speakers may refer.

Lesson 25

May I Help You?

Background Explain that it is important for students to know the proper language to use in different social situations. Tell students that they are going to practice asking for help when purchasing something in a store.

Demonstration Write the following dialogue on chart paper.

Salesperson:	*May I help you?*
Student:	*Yes, please. I'm looking for a sweatshirt.*
Salesperson:	*What size would you like?*
Student:	*Medium, please.*
Salesperson:	*They're over here.*
Student:	*Thank you. How much are they?*
Salesperson:	*Fifteen dollars and forty-five cents.*
Student:	*Thanks for your help.*

Read one line of dialogue at a time and be sure students understand what is being said and who is saying it. Then ask students to echo-read the dialogue with you one line at a time. Help them focus on intonation and pronunciation. Make sure students understand the vocabulary in the Idea Bank.

Activity Set up a table to use as a store. If you have play money, have students use it to pay and count out change.

1. Ask students to choose a partner and practice the dialogue.

2. Encourage them to place their own sweaters, sweatshirts, and gloves on their desks and use them in their role-playing, or select ideas from the Idea Bank.

3. Provide help as necessary. Repeat any words that students have difficulty pronouncing, and model intonation where appropriate. Check that they understand the meaning.

4. Let students take turns bringing their objects to the "store" at the front of the classroom and performing their dialogues at the table.

IDEA BANK

pair of shoes	belt for my father
gift for my mother/father	bottle of shampoo
toy for my brother	baseball cap

Modifications Pair less proficient English speakers with more proficient ones who will be able to support them in the role-playing.

STUDENT OBJECTIVES

- Use appropriate language
- Use accurate pronunciation
- Listen for meaning
- Make requests

TESOL Standards

- Social Language
- Culturally Appropriate Language

Additional Practice

Speaking/Writing
Students can repeat the activity using other types of purchases from the Idea Bank. Encourage them to improvise on the model dialogue.

Writing
Have students write brief store dialogues to perform with a partner.

Lesson 26

What's on the Menu?

STUDENT OBJECTIVES

- Make requests
- Use intonation and expression
- Express social courtesies

TESOL Standards

- Social Language
- Culturally Appropriate Language

Additional Practice

Listening/Speaking
You may want to provide a dialogue for buying something in a store. Write dialogue for a student and a shopkeeper, and let partners take turns performing their role-playing for the class.

Reading
Bring in take-out menus and help students use context clues to read and understand the choices to build vocabulary.

Background Explain that it is important to know the right language to use in different social situations. Display examples of real menus. Tell students that they are going to practice how to read a menu and order food in a restaurant.

Demonstration Write the following dialogue on chart paper or distribute it to the class in a handout. Choose a more advanced student to help you demonstrate.

Waiter:	*May I help you?*
Student:	*Yes, I'd like soup and a salad, please.*
Waiter:	*Would you like anything to drink?*
Student:	*Yes, I'd like a large lemonade.*

Read one line of dialogue at a time and be sure students understand what is being said and who is saying it. Then ask students to echo-read the dialogue with you one line at a time. Help them focus on intonation as well as pronunciation.

Activity Use the items in the Idea Bank to make a short menu, with pictures cut from a magazine for extra support. Read the food choices aloud together. Next, set up a table in the front of the classroom. Put a menu on the table. Bring a note pad and an apron, if available.

1. Ask students to practice reading the dialogue with a partner.

2. Encourage them to use movement and gesture to bring their role-playing to life.

3. Provide help to each pair as necessary. Model pronunciation and intonation where appropriate. Check that students understand the meaning.

4. Let students take turns sitting at the table and using the props to act out the dialogue.

Ask students to use other foods from the Idea Bank/menu to vary the dialogue.

IDEA BANK

hamburger and french fries	lo mein noodles
pizza with mushrooms	lasagna
soup and salad	spring rolls
veggie burrito	tacos

Modifications Pair beginning English speakers with more proficient students who will be able to help them in the role-playing.

Lesson 27

Special Occasions

Background Explain to students that people celebrate or acknowledge different occasions with different types of greetings.

Demonstration Draw a word web on a sheet of chart paper. Write *special occasions* in the center circle. Ask students to name important events that people celebrate. This is a good opportunity to let students share their family customs. Write them in the outer circles.

If students haven't named all the occasions in the Idea Bank, give them clues to elicit them. Talk about what each occasion stands for and how people celebrate or acknowledge it. Then tell students what they might say to someone experiencing that occasion.

Activity Invite students to play a game to familiarize themselves with the types of greetings they can use for different occasions. You will need to make two cards for each greeting card, one greeting card for each occasion in the Idea Bank. (You may wish to use a computer or have students make the cards.) The front card should include a holiday image and message, such as "On Your Wedding Day." The inside card should include the appropriate greeting.

1. Give each student one side of a greeting card. Have students read their messages and greetings.

2. Then ask students to move around the room and look for the people who have the corresponding sides of their cards.

3. When students have found their matches, have them take turns reading them to the class and explaining how they knew. Talk about what you might say to someone on each occasion.

IDEA BANK

Graduation/Congratulations!
New Year/Happy New Year!
Birthday/Happy Birthday!
Wedding/Congratulations!
Sympathy/My deepest regrets.

Modifications Give beginning English speakers cards with very little language and clear visual clues to support them in this activity.

STUDENT OBJECTIVES

- Exchange greetings
- Talk about special occasions
- Express social courtesies

TESOL Standards

- Social Language
- Culturally Appropriate Language

Additional Practice

Speaking
Write *Happy Birthday* at the top of a sheet of chart paper. Then have students take turns writing *Happy Birthday* in their first languages on the paper. Display it in the classroom. Have students refer to it to greet each other in different languages on birthdays.

Writing
Have the class make cards to celebrate events or birthdays. Focus on using appropriate terms.

Lesson 28

Sometimes, Always, Never

STUDENT OBJECTIVES

- Use time expressions
- Respond to questions nonverbally
- Identify activities

TESOL Standards

- Social Language
- Culturally Appropriate Language

Additional Practice

Listening/Speaking
Students can walk around the room and respectfully ask each other about how often they do a specific activity, such as *watch TV*, *go clothes shopping*, *eat vegetables*, etc. Have students keep a tally on paper and then share their results with the class.

Background Explain that time expressions tell how often someone does something. Tell students that there are things we do only sometimes, things that we do every day, and things that we do not do at all.

Demonstration Choose one of the time expressions from the Idea Bank: for example, *every day.* Use examples to explain the meaning of *every day.* Write *every day* on the chalkboard. Ask students to name things they do every day, such as *eat breakfast*, *brush my teeth*, *comb my hair*. Write the examples in a column beneath *every day.*

Repeat this with the other time expressions in the Idea Bank.

Activity Tell students that the class is going to work together to make a chart that tells how often students perform different activities.

1. Give each student three blank index cards and ask him or her to write a time expression from the Idea Bank on each card.

2. Name an activity: for example, *ride a bicycle.* Have students read the words on their cards and raise the cards that have a time expression that shows how often they do this activity.

3. Have students who have the same answers stand in a line, forming a human graph of the class results.

4. Count up the number of students in each group and create a paper chart of the results such as the one below.

Repeat this many times, asking students about different activities.

Activity	Sometimes	Always	Never
ride a bike	4	5	1
skateboard	3	7	0

IDEA BANK

every day	always	frequently
sometimes	often	seldom
never	once in a while	every year

Modifications Challenge more proficient English speakers to use the chart to help them talk about the kinds of activities students do every day, sometimes, often, always, seldom, or never.

(Lesson 29)

Pints and Quarts

Background Explain that in the United States, the basic measurements may differ from those that students used in their home countries. Some students will be used to the metric system and may find U.S. measures difficult. Use containers, one-inch cubes, rulers, and yardsticks to illustrate the measurements and their equivalents.

Demonstration Hold up a pint container of juice or milk. Tell students: *The container holds one pint.* Have them point to the container and repeat: *one pint.*

Place two pint containers side by side. Place a quart container next to them. Point to the container and say: *one quart.* Explain that two pints equal one quart.

Hold up a one-gallon container. Say: *one gallon.* Have students point to the container and repeat: *one gallon.* Tell students that four quarts equal one gallon.

Introduce *inch*, *foot*, and *yard* in the same way using one-inch cubes, 12-inch rulers, and yardsticks.

Activity Make multiple sets of index cards with each of the measurements. Make several sets of plus signs and equal signs on other cards. Invite students to use the cards to practice making equations.

1. Divide the class into small groups. Give each group a pile of measurement cards and a pile of plus and equal sign cards.

2. Tell students that they are going to make equations. Model a simple equation, for example: *1 pint + 1 pint = 1 quart.*

3. Encourage students to work together to make equations.

4. When they have finished, let groups take turns writing their equations on the chalkboard. Read each equation aloud. If it is incorrect, ask a volunteer to go to the chalkboard and correct it.

Continue until all the measurements have been used at least once .

IDEA BANK

pint (2 pints = 1 quart)   inch (12 inches = 1 foot)
quart (4 quarts = 1 gallon)   foot (3 feet = 1 yard)
gallon   yard

Modifications Form groups of students with mixed English proficiency so that students can support each other.

STUDENT OBJECTIVES

- Understand U.S. measurements
- Use nonverbal communication
- Work cooperatively

TESOL Standards

- Academic Language
- Social Language
- Culturally Appropriate Language

Additional Practice

Listening/Speaking
Divide the class into two groups: one group says an equation and the other uses the cards to make it. Then have the groups switch roles.

Lesson 30

Party Time

STUDENT OBJECTIVES

- Tell an original story
- Build sentences
- Use past tense verbs
- Speak clearly at an understandable rate and volume

TESOL Standards

- Social Language
- Culturally Appropriate Language

Additional Practice

Listening/Speaking

Repeat the activity using the following story starter: *Saturday is Jessica's birthday. I'm going to plan a party for her.* This will give a context in which to practice building sentences using the future tense.

Background Tell students that different cultures have different types of parties and social gatherings. This is a good time to have students share information about their cultures and traditions.

Demonstration Draw a word web on the chalkboard and label the center circle *parties.* Then invite students to talk about the types of social events that they have attended in the U.S. or another country. Encourage them to talk about things they ate at the party and things they did: for example, give gifts, etc. Add these ideas to the outer circles of the word web.

Write the questions from the Idea Bank on the board or ask questions to prompt students if necessary.

Activity Invite students to make up a collaborative story about a party or celebration.

1. Ask students to sit with you in a circle.

2. Hold up a beanbag and begin the story: for example, *Last week I went to a party.*

3. Toss the beanbag to a student and have him or her add a sentence.

4. That student then passes the beanbag to another student, and so on until everyone has had a turn to add at least one sentence to the story. Let students know that they can be creative. Their contributions do not have to be true.

5. When everyone has had a turn, wrap up the story with an appropriate ending.

> **IDEA BANK**
>
> **Where was the party?**
> **When was the party?**
> **Was the party celebrating a special occasion?**
> **Who was there?**
> **What kinds of gifts did people give?**
> **What did they eat?**
> **Did they have a good time?**

Modifications Support less proficient English speakers by allowing them to refer to the word web as they take part in the activity. For more proficient English speakers, choose one to wrap up the story with an appropriate ending.

Lesson 31

On Vacation

Background Explain to students that the tense of a verb tells you when the action takes place. Remind students that present tense tells what happens now; past tense tells what happened before now; and the future tense tells about something that hasn't yet happened but will happen some time after now.

Demonstration Show students a video, brochure, or postcards from a vacation spot. Ask them to imagine that the class has gone there. Make two sets of cards: one with the names of different verb tenses (present, past, future) and the other with familiar verbs. Use the verbs in the Idea Bank or others that students know.

Pick one card from each pile: for example, *go* and *future*. Say the future form of the verb: *will go*. Then make a sentence using the future form of the verb: for example, *I will go on vacation with the class.*

Activity Invite students to play a game to help them practice using verbs in a variety of tenses in the context of the class vacation.

1. Divide students into two groups.

2. Have a student from Group 1 pick a card from each pile.

3. The student must read the verb in the tense that is given. If necessary, he or she may consult with other students in the group before answering (e.g., present: *hear—I hear*).

4. If the verb tense is used correctly, Group 2 should use the word in a sentence about what they did on vacation (e.g., *I hear the waves breaking on the beach*). If it is not correct, Group 2 should state the correct form of the verb in the given tense and then use it in a sentence.

5. Give one point for each correct answer. Continue the game until one group reaches 10 points.

IDEA BANK

go	come	do	swim	read
visit	shop	eat	hike	relax
see	hear	buy	bike	nap

Modifications For less proficient English speakers, review each of the verbs in the three tenses (present, past, future) prior to playing the game. For more proficient English speakers, you may want to include other tenses: for example, present continuous (e.g., *I am going on vacation*) and present perfect (e.g., *This is the first time the class has gone on vacation together*).

STUDENT OBJECTIVES

- Use verb tenses
- Convey time

TESOL Standards

- Academic Language
- Social Language

Additional Practice

Listening/Speaking
For a variation on this game, you may have one group say a verb in one of the given tenses and have the other group identify the tense.

Inflectional Endings

1 RDI Book 1: Inflectional Endings

Lesson 32

Lost and Found

STUDENT OBJECTIVES

- Use possessive nouns
- Answer questions
- Speak to inform

TESOL Standards

- Academic Language
- Social Language

Additional Practice

Listening/Speaking
Have students go to the Lost and Found to ask for their missing items. By having them describe the objects, students will practice using adjectives as well as possessive nouns.

Possessive Nouns and Pronouns

2 RDI Book 2: Possessive Nouns

2 RDI Book 2: Possessive Pronouns

Background Explain that a possessive noun tells who or what owns something. Tell students that usually an *-'s* is added to a singular noun to make it possessive: for example, *Sonya's backpack.* When the noun is plural and ends in *-s*, only an apostrophe is added: for example, *the boys' books.* If the noun is plural but doesn't end in *-s*, we add *-'s:* for example, *the women's shoes.* Point out that even though the spellings are different, we always hear the /s/ or /z/ sound at the end of a possessive noun.

Demonstration Hold up a student's backpack and ask the class: *Whose backpack is this?* Help students answer: *It's Sonya's backpack.* Walk around the room, pointing to students' clothing and possessions, asking: *Whose _____ is this?*

Then ask students to choose an object, for example, a sweater, hat, or personal item, and place it on their desks where the class can see it. Have students take turns holding up their objects for the class to see. Ask volunteers to name each object and say to whom it belongs: for example, *It's Anna's hairbrush.*

Activity Invite students to play a game of "Lost and Found" in which they can practice using possessive nouns.

1. Place a box on the table and label it "Lost and Found."

2. Ask students to contribute their objects to the Lost and Found. Have them take turns holding up the object and naming it as they place it in the box.

3. Classmates should pay close attention so they can remember to whom each object belongs.

4. Pull out an object from the box and ask: *Whose _____ is this?* Students should raise their hands when they can identify it.

5. Choose a student and have him or her answer: *It's Anna's hairbrush.* If you wish, at the end of the game, you can reward the person who recognizes and identifies the most objects.

Continue removing objects until the Lost and Found box is empty.

IDEA BANK

hairbrush	sweater	jacket
backpack	toys	papers

Modifications More proficient English speakers can use possessive pronouns *(hers, his, mine, ours)* as well as possessive nouns to answer the questions.

Lesson 33

How Many?

Background Tell students that this activity focuses on identifying whether or not things can be counted. For items that we can count, such as windows, we use the word *many* to express quantity, as in: *There are many windows.* For items that we cannot count, we use the word *much,* as in: *I did not get much information from the article.*

Demonstration Write one of the words from the Idea Bank on the chalkboard: for example, *people.* Ask: *How many people are there in the classroom?* Write the question beside the word *people.* Then choose a volunteer to count and say how many people there are, using the expression: *There are (25) people in the classroom.* Repeat this with other classroom objects.

Write the word *salt* on the chalkboard. Hold up a handful of salt. Have several students put their hands out flat, and give each a pinch of salt. Ask: *How much salt is there in your hand?* Write the question beside the word *salt.* Then point to one of the students with salt in his or her hand, and have the student answer. If necessary, offer suggestions such as: *There is a lot, a little bit, or a pinch.* Ask students if they can count the number of grains of salt in their hand. Explain that *salt* is a non-count noun, or a noun that cannot be counted.

Activity Invite students to use pictures to give them hands-on practice talking about how many and how much they see.

1. Divide the class into small groups.

2. Have each group write the following questions on a sheet of paper, leaving a blank space after each question to write their answers: *How many _____ are there? How much _____ is there?*

3. Give each group a picture of a scene with multiple objects.

4. Have students write the names of each countable object under the question *How many _____ are there?* and the names of each non-countable object under the question *How much _____ is there?*

5. Then let groups take turns pointing to the objects and telling how much or how many of each object there are.

IDEA BANK			
people	sand	cars	buildings
trees	dirt	snow	

Modifications Write the following cloze sentences on the board: *There are (number) (noun)s. There is (a little/a lot of) (noun).* Beginning English speakers can use these for additional support.

STUDENT OBJECTIVES

- Use count and non-count nouns
- Answer questions
- Count objects

TESOL Standards

- Academic Language
- Social Language

Additional Practice

Reading
Write the words listed in the Idea Bank on index cards. Divide the class into two groups. Have groups take turns drawing a card, reading the word, and using it in a question with *many* or *much.* The other group answers the question.

Tongue Twisters

STUDENT OBJECTIVES

- Use accurate pronunciation
- Listen for meaning

TESOL Standards

- Social Language

Additional Practice

Listening/Speaking
Make up or find tongue twisters that use the sounds that students are studying in their phonics lessons.

Phonics

1 RDI Book 1: Phonics and Syllabication

Background Explain that a tongue twister is a group of words that have similar sounds. Saying these sounds one after the other is difficult. Most people make mistakes when they say them quickly. This is meant to be challenging and funny. Ask students to share any tongue twisters that they know in their own languages.

Demonstration Choose a tongue twister from the Idea Bank: for example, *Six slimy snails sailed silently.* Use gestures and visuals to elicit meanings of as many words of the tongue twister as possible. Teach students the tongue twister by pronouncing each word clearly and having students repeat after you chorally.

Write the following clarification strategy on the chalkboard: *Please say that again.* Encourage students to use it as necessary to understand the tongue twister you are teaching them. Once students are able to repeat the tongue twister, write it on the board.

Activity Have students teach each other tongue twisters. Prepare for this activity by writing each of the tongue twisters in the Idea Bank on an index card.

1. Ask students to find partners.

2. Give one card with a tongue twister to one student in each pair.

3. Tell students not to show their cards to their partners.

4. Have the students with the cards teach the tongue twister to their partners by reading it slowly until the partners can repeat it.

5. Remind students to use the clarification strategy as many times as necessary.

> **IDEA BANK**
>
> **Six slimy snails sailed silently.**
> **Nat's knapsack strap snapped.**
> **She sees cheese.**
> **Four furious friends fought for the phone.**
> **He threw three free throws.**
> **How many cookies could a good cook cook if a good cook could cook cookies?**

Modifications Pair beginning English-language learners with more proficient English speakers. Challenge more advanced students to make up their own tongue twisters and to practice saying them faster and faster.

Lesson 35

Cognate Cognition

Background This activity focuses on Spanish speakers. Explain that cognates are words from different languages that sound alike and mean the same thing. Sometimes students can determine the meaning of an unfamiliar word by thinking about a similar word: for example, *family/familia.* Tell students that they must be careful, however, because some words sound like cognates, but do not mean the same thing, such as *camp/campo,* the latter of which means *countryside,* not *camp.* These words are called false cognates.

Demonstration Choose one of the English words from the Idea Bank, for example, *favorite,* and write it on an index card. Hold up the card, say the word, and ask Spanish-speaking students to name a Spanish word that sounds like *favorite.* Discuss the meaning of *favorite* and *favorito* so students can be sure that they are cognates and mean the same thing. Then ask a volunteer to write *favorito* on an index card. Display the cognates side by side on the chalk ledge.

Repeat this with other words from the Idea Bank.

Activity Invite students to play a memory-matching game with cognates.

1. Shuffle the cards and place them face down on a table.

2. Have students take turns turning over two cards and reading the words to make a match. A match means an English word and its Spanish cognate.

3. When students make a match, they should hold up the words and read them for all to hear.

Continue the game until all cards have been matched.

IDEA BANK

favorite/favorito
special/especial
bilingual/bilingüe
family/familia

comic/cómico(a)
possessive/posesivo(a)
rhythm/ritmo

Modifications Ask students with more developed Spanish-language skills to name additional cognates. Be sensitive to students who know the Spanish cognates but may not know how to write them.

STUDENT OBJECTIVES

STUDENT OBJECTIVES

- Identify Spanish/English cognates
- Listen attentively

TESOL Standards

- Social Language
- Culturally Appropriate Language

Additional Practice

Listening/Speaking
Ask Spanish speakers to come to class next time with two additional Spanish cognates that they have read in a newspaper or heard at home or on the radio. Write the words on cards and add them to the memory game.

Lesson 36

Stretch and Scrunch

STUDENT OBJECTIVES

- Listen actively and attentively
- Identify phonemes
- Listen for sound recognition

TESOL Standards

- Academic Language
- Social Language

Additional Practice

Listening/Speaking
Repeat this activity, letting students take turns saying the words while their classmates stretch and scrunch.

Background Certain sounds may be very challenging for English-language learners to recognize and pronounce. *S*-blends can be especially challenging for Spanish speakers who may tend to add an *e* sound before the initial *s*-blend. Three letter *s*-blends will be challenging for speakers of many languages.

Demonstration Write the word *stretch* on the board. Stretch your arms high above your head as you say the word. Have students stretch as they repeat the word with you. Emphasize the beginning *s* sound blending into the *tr* sound. Help students say the word without placing an initial *e* sound before the *s*.

Write the word *scrunch* on the board. Crouch as you scrunch up into a little ball. Have students crouch and scrunch as they repeat the word with you. Again, help students pronounce the sounds correctly.

Activity Invite students to play a game to help them distinguish between the *str* and *scr* sounds.

1. Have students stand and form a large circle around you.

2. Say one of the *str* words from the Idea Bank. Tell students to stretch their arms high above their heads when they hear a word that begins with the *str* sound. (If students are self-conscious, they may scrunch their hands into a fist and stretch their fingers out as an alternative.)

3. Say one of the *scr* words from the Idea Bank. Tell students to scrunch up into a little ball when they hear a word that begins with the *scr* sound.

4. Say words from the Idea Bank at random. You may want to say other words that do not have these sounds to help students develop their listening skills.

5. Have students stretch when they hear a word with *str* and scrunch when they hear a word with *scr*. They should do nothing when they hear a word with neither of these sounds.

IDEA BANK

streak	stress	scrap	scream
street	strict	scramble	screen
stream	string	scrape	screw
strength	strong	scratch	scribble

Modifications Repeat this game often using other sounds that students are studying in their phonics lessons.

Lesson 37

Can a Monkey Fly?

Background Explain that *can* is a word that expresses what a person or thing is able to do. *Can* is always used with an infinitive, such as: *I can speak English.*

Demonstration Write the animals and actions from the Idea Bank on the board. Select one of the animals (e.g., *shark*), point to it, and say it aloud. Then select and point to one of the actions, such as *peel a banana*, and say it aloud. Then ask: *Can a shark peel a banana?* Shake your head, answering yourself: *No, a shark can't peel a banana.*

Point to the other animals and ask if the animal can peel a banana, and prompt students to say: *No, (the animal) cannot peel a banana.* Finally, point to the monkey and say: *Yes, a monkey can peel a banana.* Encourage students to answer in complete sentences.

Go through the animals and actions in the Idea Bank and make sure that students understand them and can pronounce them. You may want to bring photos of these animals so that all students can recognize them.

Activity Invite students to quiz their classmates on what these animals can and can't do.

1. Have students choose partners.

2. Have one student ask a "can" question. The partner listens and responds. Then have them switch roles.

3. Have the class form one large group. Then have volunteers take turns asking and answering questions.

IDEA BANK

Animals	Actions
chameleon	fly
monkey	peel a banana
shark	change color
parrot	smell blood in the water
beaver	sting
scorpion	build a dam

Modifications To support less proficient English speakers, write *Yes, it can* and *No, it can't* on the board for them to refer to as they respond to classmates' questions. Challenge proficient students to think of new questions about what these animals can or cannot do (e.g., *Can a monkey lay eggs?*).

STUDENT OBJECTIVES

• Use correct word order

• Gather information

• Ask and answer questions

• Use complete sentences

TESOL Standards

• Social Language

• Culturally Appropriate Language

Additional Practice

Writing/Reading
Extend this activity by having students write questions that relate to content-area topics they are studying (e.g., *Can a senator veto a bill? Can a liquid become a solid?*).

Lesson 38
Hoops Game

STUDENT OBJECTIVES

- Use accurate pronunciation
- Make plural nouns

TESOL Standards

- Academic Language
- Social Language

Additional Practice

Speaking
Have students repeat the game using brainstormed words from categories such as animals, sports, or other activities.

Plurals

2 RDI Book 2: Single and Plural Nouns

Background Explain that plural nouns are used to express more than one person, place, or thing.

Demonstration Review the rules for making and pronouncing plurals.

- **For words that end in /t/, /p/, and /f/, add -s, pronounced /s/** (Example: *boat, boats*).

- **For words that end in /r/, /d/, and /n/, add -s, pronounced /z/** (Example: *chair, chairs*).

- **For words that end in /s/, /sh/, /ch/, /dg/, and /x/, add -es, pronounced /iz/** (Example: *box, boxes*).

Examples of irregular plurals: *man/men, person/people, child/children, mouse/mice,* and *knife/knives.*

Then, work with students to brainstorm a list of words connected to a subject, such as basketball. Draw a picture of or pantomime each word as you give its plural. See the Idea Bank for more examples.

Activity Invite students to play a game in which they practice using plural nouns. Write the singular form of the nouns students have brainstormed, one word per card. Include some simple nouns with irregular plurals. Shuffle the cards and place in a stack.

1. Divide students into two groups. Have groups take turns choosing a card.

2. One student in Group 1 should read the singular form of the noun, being careful to pronounce it correctly. He or she may confer with the group.

3. If a student in Group 2 can say or write the correct plural form of the noun, the group "wins" the card. Play until all cards have been taken; the group with the most points wins.

IDEA BANK

Words may include:

/z/: score, fan, referee, whistle, towel, locker, cheer, band, buzzer, foul
/s/: hoop, basket, ref, lay-up, alley-oop, jump shot, shot clock /iz/: coach, bench, bus, pass

---

Modifications Draw simple pictures or use photos to support students who are less English proficient.

Lesson 39

A Picture Is Worth a Thousand Words

Background Explain to students that descriptive words and phrases tell about the color, size, and shape of objects, as well as how many or how much there is of something.

Demonstration Write the following expression on the board:

A picture is worth a thousand words.

Ask students to tell what they think it means. Help them understand that this expression means that a picture tells much more than we can when we use just a few words, or that we would have to use a lot of words to describe what a picture can show.

Ask students if they think this expression should be taken literally. Elicit that it takes a lot of words to describe something as well as a picture can, but it might not take one thousand words.

Activity Tell the class that they are going to have an opportunity to see how many words they can use to describe a picture. You will need a number of magazines with large, detailed photographs.

1. Divide the class into small groups and have each group designate a recording secretary. Display a magazine picture with a lot of details.

2. Have each group member state a picture detail and then have the secretary record it. Continue until everyone has had several turns and the group has written a long list.

3. Then have the secretaries read aloud their descriptions to the class. Count up how many descriptive words each group has written. The group with the most wins.

Repeat this activity with other pictures. Choose one of the pictures from the Idea Bank or another picture that will provide students with a variety of subjects and places to describe.

IDEA BANK
Beach scene with swimmers, surfers, and people playing
   on the beach
Ski scene with snow-covered mountains and people playing
   in the snow
Family or school scenes

Modifications Form groups with mixed English proficiencies so that students can support each other in this activity.

STUDENT OBJECTIVES

- Describe people, places, things, and events
- Use adjectives
- Understand figurative language

TESOL Standards

- Social Language
- Culturally Appropriate Language

Additional Practice

Listening/Speaking
Ask students to bring in magazines of their own. Let them take turns showing each other their pictures and describing them.

Writing
Explain the term *caption* and show students some examples of pictures with captions. Have students work in pairs to write captions for one of the pictures from the activity. Help them use descriptions, such as *bright*, *blue*, and *round*.

Lesson 40

Light As a Feather

STUDENT OBJECTIVES

- Use figurative language
- Listen for meaning

TESOL Standards

- Academic Language
- Social Language
- Culturally Appropriate Language

Additional Practice

Listening/Speaking
Have students work in pairs to write their own similes to describe things that are sweet (*as honey*), loud (*as thunder*), and bright (*as the noonday sun*). Accept all answers, but afterwards you may wish to reveal the traditional similes.

Similes

1 RDI Book 1: Figurative Language

Background Explain that similes use images to compare one thing to another. Tell students that similes generally use the words *like* or *as*, as in: *light as a feather,* for example.

Demonstration Point to a light object, such as a piece of paper, in the classroom. Toss it lightly with your fingers and say: *It's light as a feather.* Explain *light* by easily picking up something light as you say *light,* and straining to pick up something as you say *heavy.* Draw a feather on the chalkboard if necessary. Have students use the simile to describe other things that are light.

Write the similes from the Idea Bank on the chalkboard. Use gestures and pictures to explain any unfamiliar words. Then begin with *cold as ice.* Dip your finger in a glass of cold water and say: *This water is as cold as ice.* Ask students to name other things that are as cold as ice. Repeat this with the other similes.

Activity Invite students to play a matching game to practice using similes. Write the following words on index cards, one word per card: *hard, cold, ice, light, feather, hot, coals, smooth, silk, white, snow, rock.* If possible, draw a picture or pantomime to illustrate each word. You may wish to make a couple of wild cards to encourage students to be creative.

1. Shuffle the cards and place them face down on a table.

2. Let students take turns turning over two cards and reading the words to make a match. A match is two words that go together to make a simile: for example, *light* and *feather.*

3. When a student makes a match, he or she must correctly use the two words in a simile sentence. Then he or she may take the cards.

4. Another student may turn over two cards to make a match.

Continue this game until all matches have been made. You may wish to have students write the similes they create.

IDEA BANK

cold as ice	smooth as silk
light as a feather	white as snow
hot as coals	hard as a rock

Modifications You may want to write sample sentences using the similes on the board for students with limited English proficiency to refer to during the activity.

Lesson 41

Play a Game of Cell Phone

Background Explain that people have a way of talking on the phone that's not the same as talking to someone in person. Depending on the level of the students, you may wish to define some terms, including: *Who's calling?, just a moment,* and *take a message.*

Demonstration Have one of the more advanced students help you model the following phone conversation, or model it yourself by changing your voice to represent the two different people:

Answerer:	*Hello?*
Caller:	*Hi, this is Chris. Is Martin there?*
Answerer:	*I'm sorry. He's not in right now. Can I take a message?*
Caller:	*Okay, can you tell him that Chris called?*
Answerer:	*Sure, I'll let him know.*
Caller:	*Thanks!*
Answerer:	*Okay, bye!*
Caller:	*Bye!*

Activity Practice telephone talk with this update on the game of telephone. Write a phone conversation from the Idea Bank on the chalkboard or distribute it on a handout.

1. Have students form groups of four or five, each with a "caller" and an "answerer." Have students form a line with the caller at one end and the answerer at the other, with the remaining students in between.

2. Begin with a ringing sound. The answerer mimes picking up the phone and says, "Hello?" to the next student. Have that student "pass it on" to the next and so on until the message reaches the caller.

3. The caller responds with the next line of the conversation and passes it back down the line. (Note: giving the caller a gender-neutral name helps avoid embarrassment.) Repeat until the conversation is complete. Rotate students so that all get a chance to be either a caller or answerer.

> **IDEA BANK**
>
> **Hold on a minute and I'll get him/her.**
> **Would you mind calling back later?**
> **I'm sorry, could you repeat that?**

Modifications Use a shorter model for beginning students. Use a longer sample for advanced students.

STUDENT OBJECTIVES

- Understand telephone talk
- Build vocabulary
- Practice pronunciation
- Listen for verbal cues

TESOL Standards

- Social Language
- Culturally Appropriate Language

Additional Practice

Listening/Speaking
Repeat the process with other telephone conversations.

Writing
Have students practice taking phone messages based on improvised conversations.

Lesson 42

What's the Forecast?

STUDENT OBJECTIVES

- Describe weather
- Listen for meaning
- Use visuals to construct meaning

TESOL Standards

- Social Language
- Academic Language
- Culturally Appropriate Language

Additional Practice

Listening/Speaking
Introduce the seasons: winter, spring, summer, and fall. Have groups take turns describing the weather in each of those seasons. Support students who come from countries where the seasons may be different from those in your area.

Reading
Show students weather information presented in a newspaper. Help them find and read the weather forecasts for their countries of origin.

Background Explain to students that it is important that they understand weather forecasts so they can be prepared for different kinds of weather. Ask students about their experience with radio or TV weather reports.

Demonstration Choose a weather word from the Idea Bank: for example, *sunny.* Draw a sun on the board and say: *It's sunny.* Repeat this with other words in the Idea Bank. Use pictures and gestures to convey the meanings of *cloudy, foggy, rainy, snowy,* and *windy.*

Point to a picture of snowy weather. Place your arms across your chest and shiver. Say: *It's cold.* Use a picture of a beautiful spring day to show *warm,* and another of a hot summer day with people swimming or doing other activities in the water to show *hot.*

Activity Tell students that they are going to have an opportunity to make their own weather reports and to identify weather conditions. You will need pictures that show different weather conditions.

1. Divide the class into small groups.

2. Give each group a picture of different weather conditions.

3. Have groups work together to write a brief weather report about their pictures: for example, *Today we had a perfect fall day—with sunny, warm, and dry conditions.*

4. Collect the pictures and display them along a ledge.

5. Let groups take turns reading aloud their weather report.

6. Choose volunteers to point to the picture that the weather report describes.

IDEA BANK

sunny	windy	snowy
rainy	cloudy	drizzle
warm	hot	
foggy	cold	

Modifications Students with limited English proficiency may not be prepared to give a weather report, but they can participate in the activity by pointing to the pictures of the weather conditions described. Challenge more advanced students to include more detailed information or to make a forecast for the rest of the week.

Lesson 43
Meaning Match

Background Explain to students that some words in English have more than one meaning and that the only way to know which meaning is intended is by paying attention to the context. The context is the information around the word that gives clues to its meaning.

Demonstration Choose a word from the Idea Bank—for example, *fair*—and make one card for each different meaning (*just; a carnival*). Acknowledge that there are other meanings, such as pretty. Show students a picture or describe a county fair. Explain that a fair is a public showing of animals or other products and often includes shows, contests, and other entertainment.

Write sentences that reflect the two meanings on large sentence strips, leaving a blank for the multiple-meaning word.

The teacher's decision was _____ to both students.

Our school has a book _____ every year.

Choose a volunteer to place the word card with the correct definition for *fair* in the blank and then to read the sentence aloud. Repeat this with other words from the Idea Bank.

Activity Invite students to play a game using sentence strips for each multiple-meaning word.

1. Divide the class into two groups. Give one group the sentence strips. Give the other group the word cards for each multiple-meaning word.

2. The first group reads the sentence aloud. The second group provides the word to fill in the blank.

3. When groups are done, say one of the multiple-meaning words and have groups take turns reading their sentences with that word.

4. To confirm meaning, have students act out, role-play, or discuss the meaning of each word in its context.

IDEA BANK

spring (Look at the spring flowers. In the morning we will
    spring into action.)
park (Did you park the car? I want to go to the park.)
kind (I like that kind of music. She was kind.)
fair (The decision was fair. Our school held a career fair.)
hard (The test was hard. The dirt became hard in the sun.)

Modifications Challenge more proficient English speakers to write the words in sentences that show their meaning.

STUDENT OBJECTIVES

- Use multiple-meaning words
- Use context to determine meaning
- Complete cloze sentences
- Work cooperatively

TESOL Standards

- Academic Language
- Social Language

Additional Practice

Speaking
Repeat the activity with other multiple-meaning words such as *left*, *right*, and *stamp*.

Multiple-Meaning Words

1 RDI Book 1: Multiple-Meaning Words

Lesson 44
You're Invited

STUDENT OBJECTIVES

- Use accurate pronunciation
- Extend invitations
- Accept and decline invitations

TESOL Standards

- Social Language
- Culturally Appropriate Language

Additional Practice

Listening/Speaking

Challenge students to use their imaginations to create other dialogues in which they extend and accept or decline invitations. You may wish to introduce concepts such as *RSVPing, taking a rain check*, etc.

Writing

Bring in invitations and show students how to write invitations to social events.

Background Explain that it is important to know the proper language to use in different social situations. Ask students if they have ever been invited to someone's home for dinner or to a party. Tell them that they are going to learn how to extend invitations and how to accept or decline invitations from others.

Demonstration Write the following dialogue on chart paper or distribute it on a handout.

Mrs. Gomez:	*Would you like to stay and have dinner with us?*
Student:	*No, I can't. I have to go home and do my homework. But thank you for asking.*
Mrs. Gomez:	*You're very welcome. Perhaps some other time.*

Explain that the student is visiting a friend's house. The friend's mother is inviting the student to stay and have dinner with the family. Read one line at a time. Make sure students understand what is being said. Have students choral-read the dialogue with you, being careful to focus on intonation as well as pronunciation.

Activity Invite students to role-play scenes in which invitations are extended and accepted or declined.

1. Brainstorm scenarios such as those found in the Idea Bank and write them on strips of paper. Put the strips of paper in a bag.

2. Ask students to choose a partner; each pair should then draw a strip from the bag.

3. Have each pair practice a short dialogue based on the scenario they have chosen. Encourage students to substitute other invitations in place of *stay and have dinner with us*.

4. Provide help as necessary. Repeat any words that students have difficulty pronouncing and model intonation when appropriate.

> **IDEA BANK**
>
> Accepting an invitation
> Inviting someone to a party or dinner
> Politely declining an invitation
> Offering to bring something
> Accepting an invitation, but suggesting another time

Modifications Pair beginning English speakers with more proficient students who can support them in the role-playing.

Lesson 45

News Flash

Background Explain to students that to be understood in English one needs to know which words to emphasize or stress. It is important to emphasize informational words, such as proper nouns and nouns, rather than connecting words, such as *in, the, about, of,* and so on.

Demonstration Read the following sentence from a sample news report in the style of a newscaster:

A <u>flood</u> <u>warning</u> was <u>declared</u> this <u>morning</u>.

Repeat slowly, clapping the rhythm of the words. Write the words on the chalkboard. Underline the stressed words. Point out the importance of proper emphasis and phrasing in having your words understood.

To help students understand the importance of proper word stress, reread the sentence, emphasizing the words *A, was,* and *this.* Talk about how the sentence loses its meaning.

Activity Write three sample sentences on the board. Invite students to listen attentively as you read the words. They are to echo by clapping the rhythm.

1. Read the first sentence from the Idea Bank aloud, placing emphasis on key words.

2. Have students clap the rhythm of the sentence as you point to the words on the board.

3. Repeat the process with the two remaining sample sentences.

For more practice, use short sentences from actual news articles.

> **IDEA BANK**
>
> **Malik Bryant scored 24 points last night.**
> **Mayor Chavez led the parade.**
> **The new Fairfield library opened this week.**

Modifications Challenge proficient English speakers by having them lead the rest of the class in identifying stressed words. Support less proficient English speakers by helping them identify key words in a sentence.

STUDENT OBJECTIVES

- Listen attentively
- Recognize spoken rhythms

TESOL Standards

- Social Language
- Culturally Appropriate Language

Additional Practice

Listening
Give students written copies of the sentences from the Idea Bank. Have them underline accented words as you read and reread them aloud.

Writing/Reading
Extend the activity by having pairs of students write their own lead sentences from the news. Have students work with partners to read the leads. Have them identify and then underline all the stressed words.

Lesson 46

Easily Confused Words

STUDENT OBJECTIVES

- Use accurate pronunciation
- Distinguish easily confused words

TESOL Standards

- Academic Language
- Social Language

Additional Practice

Speaking
Repeat this activity with other easily confused words such as *adapt/adopt*, *precede/proceed*, *sit/set*, and *through/thorough*.

Background Explain that in English there are some words that look and sound very much like other words. These words can easily be confused, so it's important to know the difference between the sounds, spellings, pronunciations, and meanings of these word pairs.

Demonstration Write one of the word pairs from the Idea Bank on the chalkboard: for example, *affect* and *effect*. Point to each word and pronounce it clearly. Have students repeat the words with you. Then explain that *affect* is a verb and it means *to influence* or *change*. Tell students that *effect* is a noun and it means *the result or consequence of something.* Challenge volunteers to use each word in a sentence, for example:

> **If I don't study, it could affect my grades.**

> **I hope my studying will have a good effect on my grades.**

Repeat this with other word pairs in the Idea Bank.

Activity Invite students to play a game in which they practice distinguishing easily confused words.

1. Divide the class into two teams.

2. Define a pair of words from the Idea Bank. Display a coin and tell students that heads will be one word (such as *affect*) and tails the other (such as *effect*).

3. Flip the coin and ask Team 1 to come up with a sentence using the word for that coin side. Have a volunteer write the sentence on the board and read it aloud.

4. Ask Team 2 to come up with a sentence using the remaining word in the pair. Have a volunteer write the sentence below the first one and read it aloud.

5. Repeat using all the words in the Idea Bank.

Continue until all matches have been made.

> ### IDEA BANK
>
> | | |
> |---|---|
> | affect/effect | lay/lie |
> | breath/breathe | then/than |
> | all ready/already | desert/dessert |
> | emigrate/immigrate | lose/loose |

Modifications Form groups with mixed English proficiencies so students can support each other in this activity.

Lesson 47

Act Out Idioms

Background Explain that an idiom is an expression that has a meaning that is different from the meanings of the individual words that make it up.

Demonstration Choose one of the idiomatic phrases from the Idea Bank: for example, *hit the ceiling*. Write it on the chalkboard. Use gestures and movement to convey the literal meanings of each of the words. Ask students to guess what they think the figurative meaning might be. Tell them that to *hit the ceiling* means *to become extremely angry*. Explain that this refers to someone heating up and exploding, like a steam kettle or pressure cooker. Challenge students to name situations in which someone might *hit the ceiling*. Then help them use the word in a sentence.

Continue with the other idioms in the Idea Bank.

Activity Invite students to play a game in which they act out the feelings or perceptions conveyed by the idioms.

1. Write the idioms on strips of paper, one idiom per paper strip, and place them in a bag.

2. Choose a volunteer to pick a strip from the bag, read the idiom, and act it out.

3. Classmates should identify the emotion that the student is trying to convey. Have them raise their hands when they know the idiom that expresses that emotion.

4. The first student to use the idiom correctly can pick the next strip from the bag and act it out.

IDEA BANK

to sweat it out (to worry intensely)
to hit the ceiling (to become extremely angry)
to be nuts about (to be extremely enthusiastic)
to be down in the dumps (to be sad, depressed)
to be a pain in the neck (to be annoying)

Modifications Write the idioms and their meanings on the strips to support beginning English speakers.

STUDENT OBJECTIVES

- Understand idioms.
- Use nonverbal communication.
- Use slang.

TESOL Standards

- Social Language
- Culturally Appropriate Language

Additional Practice

Listening/Speaking
Divide the class into two groups. Have one group pick a strip and tell the meaning of the idiom on it. The other group should say the idiom that expresses that meaning.

Idioms

1 RDI Book 1: Idioms

Tone Changes Everything

STUDENT OBJECTIVES

- Ask and answer questions
- Use inflection to convey meaning
- Listen to inflection to determine meaning

TESOL Standards

- Social Language
- Culturally Appropriate Language

Additional Practice

Listening/Speaking
Working in pairs, students should take turns making statements or asking questions. The partners who listen should be able to identify questions, statements, or words being stressed to change meanings.

Background Explain that inflection describes the way we say a sentence. A statement usually has an even pitch or tone of our voice. When we ask a question, we often raise the pitch at the end.

Demonstration Say: *You went there,* using an even pitch. Tell students that this is a statement. Then ask: *You went there?,* raising your voice to indicate a question. Tell students that this is a question. Finally, ask: *You went THERE?,* and explain that stressing a certain word can change the meaning, in this case indicating disbelief that you went to this particular place.

Say the statement: *She went to the store,* maintaining an even tone. Ask students whether you are making a statement or asking a question. Have them repeat the statement with you. Then repeat the same words, but this time raising your voice to indicate a question. Have students ask the question with you. Help them hear the difference in the inflection. Finally, ask: *SHE went to the store?* and have students repeat it. Ask students how this question differs from the previous question. They should understand that it expresses disbelief or doubt that this particular person went to the store.

Continue with other sentences in the Idea Bank.

Activity This activity will give students an opportunity to practice distinguishing statements from questions based on inflection.

1. Ask students to choose partners, one per student.

2. Have the partners work together to write a dialogue that includes a statement expressed in the three different ways using tone and inflection to vary the meaning.

3. Invite the pairs to read their dialogues to the class.

IDEA BANK

Mom's out.	Mom's out?	Mom's OUT?
She's at the mall.	She's at the mall?	SHE'S at the mall?
She lost the car.	She lost the car?	She LOST the car?

Modifications For more proficient English speakers, you may introduce the concept of sarcasm as an additional case of how tone changes meaning.

Lesson 49

Play Catch With Proverbs

Background Explain that a proverb is a wise saying that is commonly known. Many proverbs use figurative language, i.e., they don't mean exactly what the words say. (Note: Beginning English learners may not able to comprehend the full meaning of these proverbs but will benefit by being able to recognize these sayings as such. With repeated exposure, they will gain a deeper understanding.)

Demonstration Say this proverb: *The pen is mightier than the sword.* Help students understand the proverb by showing pictures of a sword and a pen or drawing them on the board. Pantomime strength by making a muscle. Then point to the pen. Pantomime a weaker muscle and then point to the sword. Elicit from students that the pen is stronger. Help students understand the nonliteral meaning of the proverb. Explain that force can control people, but words can change how they think. Ask students to contribute any wise sayings that they know from their own languages and cultures and translate them for the class, if possible.

Activity Practice proverbs with students using call and response.

1. Demonstrate another proverb from the Idea Bank—for example, *time is money*—by drawing a clock, an equal sign, and a dollar sign on the board. Help students understand the proverb by having them state the meaning in their own words.

2. Practice saying it together chorally. Signal one half of the group to say *Time is . . .* Signal the other half of the group to finish the proverb. Give everyone a chance to practice both parts.

3. Toss a crumpled piece of paper or soft foam ball to one student, saying *Time is . . .* and cue the student to respond with the rest of the proverb. (*money*)

4. Have that student begin *Time is . . .* and toss the ball to another student, who then finishes the proverb, and so on.

IDEA BANK

Time is money.
Let sleeping dogs lie.
Don't cry over spilled milk.
People who live in glass houses shouldn't throw stones.

Modifications Work with more advanced students on the nonliteral meanings of the proverbs and challenge them by introducing longer proverbs into the game.

STUDENT OBJECTIVES

- Recognize proverbs
- Practice pronunciation
- Listen for verbal cues
- Build vocabulary

TESOL Standards

- Culturally Appropriate Language

Additional Practice

Writing
Repeat the activity with idiomatic expressions, such as *time flies*, *catch you later*, and *don't let the cat out of the bag*. Students may enjoy writing a proverb on a piece of drawing paper and illustrating it.

Idioms

1 RDI Book 1: Idioms

Lesson 50

What's the News?

Additional Practice

Speaking
Repeat this activity, substituting a weather forecast for the news report.

Background Explain that newscasters must speak clearly so that all listeners can understand the news they are reporting. Ask students to name other people who must speak especially clearly to provide information. These may include weather forecasters and teachers.

Demonstration Tape-record a news program from the radio or television, or make up your own news feature. Write the script on a sheet of poster paper or distribute it as a handout. Display the script of the newscast as you play the tape, or read it with a loud voice, clear pronunciation, and expressive inflections. Make sure everyone understands the newscast.

Then ask students to echo-read the newscast line by line with you. Help them pronounce difficult words and encourage them to imitate your intonation. Continue one line at a time until students have practiced reading the entire script.

Activity Give students an opportunity to prepare and perform their own newscasts.

1. Give each student a short news article or have them select one of the suggestions from the Idea Bank.

2. Ask students to use the article or suggestion to write a simple newscast. Provide assistance as necessary.

3. Give students time to practice reading their newscasts independently. Ask them to focus on clear pronunciation and expressive inflections. Then have students select partners.

4. Have one partner read his or her newscast. The other partner should coach him or her on proper pronunciation and appropriate intonation. Then ask partners to switch roles.

5. When everyone has had time to practice, let volunteers take turns performing their newscasts for classmates.

> ### IDEA BANK
>
> The school soccer team won the game against _____.
> _____ won the award for best movie of the year.
> The rap group _____ is going to perform in town.
> There was a parade up Main Street to celebrate _____.

Modifications Allow students to record themselves practicing their newscasts. This will allow them to hear how they sound and to self-correct.

How to Build Community

Community Builders are engaging activities that help students get started listening and speaking with one another. Ideally, they should be used at the beginning of the school year to build familiarity and a sense of community. Follow these suggestions for using each activity.

All About Me Interview

1. Make multiple copies of the **All About Me Interview, page 72.**

2. Have students work with a partner.

3. Explain the term *interviewer*. Designate one student in each pair as the interviewer and give that student the interview form.

4. Have interviewers write their partners' names at the top of the page and then their own names.

5. Explain that the interviewer will ask questions based on the categories on the chart. For example: *How many people are there in your family?* The interviewer then would record the answer in the box labeled *Family.*

6. When all the boxes have been filled in, have partners switch roles. Distribute an interview form to the new interviewer.

7. When completed, ask each interviewer to tell the rest of the class two things about the person interviewed.

8. Repeat the activity at another time with different pairs.

I'm Looking for Someone Who . . .

1. Copy and distribute **I'm Looking For Someone Who . . . , page 73.**

2. Model how to read an item listed in the *Category* column and write the answer in the *My Favorite* column. For example: *My favorite animal is a tiger.* Write *tiger* in the *My Favorite* column.

3. Then have students fill in the entire *My Favorite* column with their own preferences.

4. Explain to students that they will now try to find other students in class who share the same favorite items as they do. Model how students might approach one another to find out their preferences.

5. Have students record the names of the students who share the same interest in the last column.

6. Ask them to determine the student with whom they share the most interests.

All About Me Interview

Date _____

Interviewed by _____

Family	**Friends**

Favorite Food	**Favorite Movie**

Favorite Place	**Favorite Hobby**

Favorite Sport	**Favorite Subject**

Name _____

Date _____

I'm Looking for Someone Who . . .

Category	My Favorite	Someone Who Likes It, Too
Animal		
Book		
Movie		
Clothing		
Fruit		
Hero		
Hobby		
Vegetable		
Holiday		
Music Group		
Dessert		
Sport		
TV Show		

Activity Tracking Chart

Activity	Date	Notes
1. Drag Your Mouse		
2. Memory Game		
3. Talking About Books		
4. Feeling Fine		
5. Command Performance		
6. Ten Questions		
7. Thirty, Thumbs, *and Other Words With /th/*		
8. Same Story		
9. Blue Jeans and Red Socks		
10. Number Bingo		
11. Word Jumbles		
12. What's the Scoop?		
13. Rhyme Scheme		
14. Pleased to Meet You		
15. At the Market		
16. Three Cheers!		
17. Teens and Tens		

Name _____

Activity Tracking Chart

Activity	Date	Notes
18. *Guess Who?*		
19. *Guess What?*		
20. *Animal Chains*		
21. *Echo With a Twist*		
22. *Getting From Here to There*		
23. *Bragging Rights*		
24. *Scheduling Time*		
25. *May I Help You?*		
26. *What's on the Menu?*		
27. *Special Occasions*		
28. *Sometimes, Always, Never*		
29. *Pints and Quarts*		
30. *Party Time*		
31. *On Vacation*		
32. *Lost and Found*		
33. *How Many?*		
34. *Tongue Twisters*		

Activity Tracking Chart

Activity	Date	Notes
35. Cognate Cognition		
36. Stretch and Scrunch		
37. Can a Monkey Fly?		
38. Hoops Game		
39. A Picture Is Worth a Thousand Words		
40. Light As a Feather		
41. Play a Game of Cell Phone		
42. What's the Forecast?		
43. Meaning Match		
44. You're Invited		
45. News Flash		
46. Easily Confused Words		
47. Act Out Idioms		
48. Tone Changes Everything		
49. Play Catch With Proverbs		
50. What's the News?		

Index

(Continued on next page)